GAMES (& other stuff) FOR GROUP
·BOOK 1·

REVISED & EXPANDED

by Chris Cavert & Friends

Published by:

Wood & Barnes Publishing
2717 NW 50th
Oklahoma City, OK 73112
(405) 946-0621

Cover Art by Chris Cavert.
Copyediting & Design by Ramona Cunningham

Emotions Poster © 1990 Wellness Reproductions & Publishing, Inc.
800-669-9208 Used with permission.

Printed in the United States of America
Oklahoma City, Oklahoma
ISBN # 1-885473-39-7

To order copies of this book, please call:
Jean Barnes Books
800-678-0621

—— PLAY FOR PEACE ——

All royalties from this publication will be donated to *Play for Peace*.

PURPOSE

Play for Peace brings children of conflicting cultures together through cooperative play to promote positive relationships among people who have a history of inter-cultural tension. By bringing children with unique backgrounds, values and beliefs together through the seemingly simple act of play, seeds of compassion are sown for a more peaceful today and tomorrow.

OBJECTIVES

- To promote positive relationships among children from cultures in conflict.
- To create a non-threatening environment, free from fear, where children can experience the joy of play.
- To influence the behavior of adults through the positive example of children at play.
- To draw positive global attention to areas in the world which experience negative media exposure.

VISION

Play for Peace is a process of community building. Rather than being an event or program, it is the creation of ongoing learning partnerships that frees each child to build positive life-long connections with others. Especially among people with a history of inter-cultural tension, cooperative play is one of the few bridges that promote positive cross-cultural relationships.

It is the intent of *Play for Peace* that children throughout the world will someday have the opportunity to experience the ways in which we are all connected, develop compassion for others, and share laughter with people that are "different" from themselves.

Play for Peace has already been active in Chicago working together with African-American and Latino communities; in Israel with Muslim and Christian groups; in Bosnia-Herzegovina, Croatia, Serbia; in Central America; and in South Africa. For more information on how you can support *Play for Peace*, write:

Play for Peace
P.O. Box 6205
Buffalo Grove, IL 60089 U.S.A.
(847)-520-1444
info@playforpeace.org

Acknowledgments

This book of activities could not have been possible without the contributions of my friends and colleagues.

I want to thank my true friends, Tim Green and Brian Brolin,
for their efforts and contributions to this book.
To Karl Rohnke, the gamesman who inspired me.
Thanks also go out to Sam Sikes, Tim Finkbeiner, Frank Harris,
Jim Cain, Barry Jolliff, William M. Hazel, Susana G. Acosta,
Irvington Publishers, Barbra McDowell and Clifford Knapp.
Your contributions will touch many lives.

"Together We Will Make A Difference!"

Special Thanks
to my wonderful mother,
Mary Sue Cavert,
who taught me how to be patient.

&

To Mony and the rest of the
Wood 'N' Barnes staff for
putting their special touch to this book
and making it available to us
all over the world.

(let us not forget the legal stuff)

Disclaimer

Improper use of this information could result in injury. Please seek out a qualified professional to train you in any area you are not fully prepared for. The reader assumes all risk and liability for any loss or damage that may result from the use of the information in this book.

CONTENTS

"What can I do to get my group to open up and talk?" I have been asked this question by many group leaders looking for a better way. **Games (& other stuff) for Group** could be your answer.

This book contains 37 different activities, from stories to games, over 200 "What would it be like....?" questions, and (the new section for '99) over 250 "Are You More Like...?" doublets to assist you in charging up your group. If I were to set an age range for the activities, it would be 12 and older. This doesn't mean your creativity can't change them enough to work for younger ages. All the activities (except for a few I could not resist adding) last about 10 - 15 minutes. Each activity is a catalyst for topical discussions. Some of the topics include expressing emotions, learning names, effects of rumors, gender issues, trust, honor, following directions, creative thinking, frustration, and communication.

There are five areas of choice within this book. The activities (Section One) are of a physical nature. Most of the activities include a small prop of some sort (easy to find or make). I have found that props often stimulate interest in participation. This interest can roll over into the topic discussion at hand. Each activity includes a list of topic observations and questions to get you started.

The "What would it be like...?" questions (Section Two) can be used to break the ice in your group. Select certain questions related to issues you would like to discuss or just pick questions at random. I have used these questions success-fully with many different age groups.

Teaching Tales (Section Three) are one to two page stories with a message wo-ven into the lines. These tales create a visual image of certain issues that may relate to members of your group. Through the characters in the story, group members can express similar situations. Each tale has a list of discussion ques-tions to facilitate learning.

Minute Mysteries (Section Four) are short story-riddles that contain an issue to discuss with your group. The mysteries involve the entire group asking ques-tions to solve a problem. Through this process, group members can develop lat-eral and creative thinking skills. The answers are found through group effort and persistence - two additional topics for a useful discussion. Each mystery also includes a set of questions to help you explore the topic at hand.

Finally, there is a collection of options that will challenge a group to decide "Are You More Like...?" this or that (Section Five). Making choices is not an easy thing sometimes. Once a choice is made it might even be harder to explain. These word pairs are a fun way to think about why we choose what we do and, at the same time, help us to discover a little more about ourselves.

There is one thing I would like to share about using this book. It has to do with "the blank pages." Use this space for tips, notes, and ideas on the hows, whys, and what fors. I would love to hear about all the creative applications you come up with. Great stuff can help other great people like yourself - please pass it on!

Most of the **Games (& other stuff) for Group** in this book comes from the **E.A.G.E.R. Curriculum**, by Chris Cavert. The Curriculum includes over 200 events and 187 variations of **E**xperiential **A**ctivities, **G**ames and **E**ducational **R**ecreation. The Curriculum is designed for educators interested in Adventure-Based Counseling and Experiential Programming ideas.

Please present the information in this book with a spirit of adventure and fun. Making your group a fun place to be will surely encourage participation. Adding some adventure (an undertaking involving the unknown) can create curiosity and motivate participation.

Our work is important to the lives of many people (even when they don't seem to think so). It is our job to find out what can light the fire inside. These **Games (& other stuff) for Group** have really helped me. I hope they can help you too. Enjoy!

PRESENTING & PROCESSING

The ultimate goal of an experiential facilitator is to guide participants through their own discovery of new experiences. From these new experiences, participants can learn how to relate new skills, ideas, and behaviors to future life situations.

To do this, it will help to have some knowledge of presenting and processing games and activities. Some established procedures include the "Adventure Wave Plan," outlined in **Islands of Healing** by Schoel, Prouty, & Radcliff (1988) and the "Experiential Learning Cycle," by Nadler & Luckner (1992). Another common approach to presenting and processing is "Experience...What?," "So What?," and "Now What?"

Proper ground work is important for the "Experience." First you will want to choose an activity that suits the objective of your session. It should be appropriate for the ability and age of the group, and fit within the limitations of your program facilities. Next, you will want to give clear instructions and safety guidelines, then provide ample time for questions before the activity starts. As the group begins, you become the watchful facilitator, keeping the activity safe at all times.

"What?" happens is up to the group. Some facilitators choose to ask questions about what is happening during the activity. Other facilitators wait until the end to ask. Some facilitators ask during and after an activity. This choice is ultimately up to you.

"So what?" were you feeling or experiencing during the activity is next. This is where skills, behaviors, emotions, and feedback are encouraged. Keeping the discussion safe for all individuals will increase the bonding potential of the group and develop the trust levels needed to take future risks.

To complete the cycle, "Now what?" are you going to do with any new information that you have obtained? This stage pushes learning into the next activity and, with hope, into real life situations. Making the learning relevant to future life situations is where behavior change starts.

The hardest part of the experiential process is not giving out solutions to problems. As adults it is easy to tell someone how to do something, especially if we have a solution. However, more knowledge is gained by self discovery than lecture. Let the group discover what is in the treasure chest. You can provide the key with thoughtful questions.

Preparation, facilitation, and processing are skills enhanced through time. If you are not satisfied with the way you approached a problem, use the situation

as a learning "Experience...What" happened? So "What" did you learn from it?
"Now What" are you going to do next time? The process is not just for the
group. This is what experiential education is all about. There is always something to learn.

I encourage you to obtain more information about the Experiential Process.
Several excellent books and training programs are listed in the Reference Sec-
tion and in the Appendix. A good teacher is also a good learner. Now on to the
Adventure!

SAMPLE PROCESSING QUESTIONS

I have included a few questions to help you "get the ball rolling" so to speak. There are also questions included with most of the activities within this book. I have found it difficult to plan the exact questions I will ask during an activity, because I never know what the group will pull from their experience. Generally, I plan a few questions, then adapt to what the group needs at the time.

1. Let's recap what just happened here. What did you see?
2. Who can share something that was helpful during the activity?
3. Who can share something that wasn't helpful?
4. Did everyone express his or her opinion when a choice was available?
5. What were some effective forms of communication that you used in completing this task? Ineffective forms of communication?
6. How could you improve your own way of communicating?
7. What are some specific examples of when the group cooperated during the activity?
8. How did cooperative behavior lead to the successful completion of the task?
9. What can you do to produce a cooperative environment?
10. What effect did planning have on your activity?
11. How effective was the group at solving problems during the activity?
12. What are the similarities and differences between the ways in which you have approached solving problems here, and the way you approach them at home or at school?
13. What would need to change in order to enhance your problem-solving ability?
14. What were the behaviors that you would describe as demonstrating leadership?
15. Was it difficult to assume a leadership role in this group? Why?
16. What are the characteristics and qualities of a good leader?
17. Do you consider yourself a good follower? Was this an important role during the activity?
18. What are the characteristics of a good follower?
19. What was difficult about being a follower?
20. Did you criticize yourself or put yourself down during the activity?
21. What did you say to yourself?
22. Do you usually get upset with yourself when you make a mistake or do not achieve perfection?
23. What could you say to yourself to counteract the put-down messages?
24. What were some ways in which you were successful during the activity?
25. What self-messages did you give yourself when you were successful?
26. What are some examples of when you gave feedback during the session?
27. Is it hard for you to give someone feedback? Why?
28. Was there a time during the session when you would have liked to give someone feedback but didn't? Would you be willing to give that person

feedback now?
29. How did you express appreciation for another person's actions during the session?
30. What are some appreciations that you did not express?
31. How can you improve your skills in giving and receiving feedback?
32. What was happening to you emotionally as you experienced the activity?
33. How did you feel about the activity?
34. What did you think about what was happening during the activity?
35. Were there any significant issues during the activity?
36. How were the issues handled?
37. What was the outcome?
38. How might the issues have been avoided?
39. Has this, or something similar ever happened to you or someone you know?
40. What are some ways the issues could have been dealt with more appropriately?
41. What are some of the significant differences you have noticed among group members?
42. In what specific instances did being different help or hinder the group during the activity?
43. How did these differences strengthen the group?
44. What would the group be like if there were very few differences among the group members?
45. What did you learn about yourself?
46. What did you learn about the others in your group?
47. What new questions do you have about yourself and others?
48. What did you do today that you were particularly proud of?
49. How can you use what you learned today in other situations?
50. What skill are you working to improve?
51. Was your behavior today typical of the way you usually act in a group? Explain.
52. Would you do anything differently if you were starting the activity again with this group?
53. Is there anything you would like to say to the group?

(others)

SECTION ONE

ACTIVITIES

THOUGHTS · NOTES · REVELATIONS

NEEDS: 1 roll of <u>unused</u> toilet paper and space for a small circle.

PROCEDURE: Sit in a comfortable circle and pass the roll of toilet paper around with these directions, "Take as many squares of toilet paper as you think you will need. Then pass the roll to the next person." "How many you need for what?" is always the question. I will often just say, "For whatever." Try to brush off the question as best as possible. Observe what happens. The reactions may have to be addressed if they are too disruptive. Some people need more information and have a hard time moving on without it. How can you help the process move on without telling any more about the activity?

If players choose not to take any tissue squares, that's okay - for now. Once everyone has had the roll, explain that you would like each person to tell the group a quality about themselves for each square of TP (double-ply squares need only count as one response). Encourage responses beyond the superficial (i.e. "I'm wearing red shoes today"). If there were individuals who did not take any squares the first time, offer the roll to them after others have gone. I always play this one so the group can get to know a little more about me!

Note: If the people in your group have never experienced this type of "sharing themselves" with others, they might find it hard to "qualify" themselves. After this activity, you might want to follow up with "My Personal Strengths Sheet," found in **Games (& other stuff) for Group•Book 2** (see Resources for how to get your copy). It is a listing of over 100 qualities you can work through and define for your group. Maybe someone is "assertive" but doesn't know it yet.

OBSERVATIONS/QUESTIONS:
- What was the comfort level of individuals?
- Did anyone have a hard time saying things about themselves?
- Were the qualities outside or inside qualities?
- Why do you think it's hard to talk about yourself?
- Is what you said about yourself what YOU believe or what others have said about you?
- Can these qualities change? How?
- Can anyone name a quality for each person in the group?
- Do all of us share one similar quality?
-
(others) •

VARIATIONS:
- Try this one with, M&Ms®. See how many they take. Do players save enough for everyone?

OTHER **I**DEAS:

GUESS WHO

NEEDS: Each group member will need a pencil and a 3" x 5" note card.

PROCEDURE: Hand out the pencils and note cards. Spend a few minutes and have each person write on the card as many unique things about themselves as they can think of. This could be special hobbies, skills, places of travel, family members, favorite things and so on. Have them print their name on the bottom of the card. When everyone has finished, collect all the cards and pencils.

At random, read each card out loud without revealing the person's name. I have done this a couple of ways. Have each person in the group pick a card to read (put the card back if it's you - or not!) or I read them each myself. I've even done some of both. If someone doesn't want to read, I read for them (reading by CHOICE).

After each card is read, ask each player to look around the group and, in their own head (this means, don't blurt out a name - this is hard for some people - another work-on - it's just crazy how this stuff works!! - now I'm rambling!?), guess who the card is about. You could guess out loud, but I have found it to be more comfortable with groups if done silently. After several seconds say the name. Let any immediate reactions take place, then move on to the next card.

This is a good way to discover commonalities within the group without making the group members talk. There are times when this is a good way to start.

OBSERVATIONS/QUESTIONS:
- Were there any correct guesses?
- How did you know it was that person?
- Was anyone surprised about any of the group members' descriptions?
- Did anyone in the group share similar experiences with you?
- Would you like to ask any questions about any of the descriptions?
- Is there something anyone would like to share that they forgot to put on their card?
- How can you find out more about the people in our group?
-
-

(others)

OTHER IDEAS:

PICK YOUR BRAIN

Thanks to Barbra McDowell.

NEEDS: One commercial Pick-Up Sticks® game (found in most toy stores), or you could use 25 colored straws (5 different colors - 6 red, 6 green, 6 yellow, 6 blue, and 1 black - the "helper" stick).

PROCEDURE: Prepare a short list of questions - at least six for each color but black (you only need a few). I like to choose categories that are relevant to the present situations of the group. For example: sports, school, dating, family, friends, and feelings. Let the players know what the categories are and what color stick is related to that category. (I have provided a sample list on page 14.)

Follow the rules for a regular game of Pick-Up Sticks® (or Spellicans® which originated in China). Decide on the order of play. The last person in the order gathers up all the sticks in one hand (holding them vertically) and drops them on the floor from a height of about 6"-8". Now the first player in the order attempts to remove a stick from the pile without moving any of the other sticks. Once a player starts to pick up a stick she is not permitted to move another stick.

If a player successfully removes a stick from the pile, she is obligated (but not forced) to answer a question from the related list. (I go down each color list in order - for simplicity. If you have more questions than sticks, a player may pass to a different question). You may see players avoiding easier sticks in order to elude a certain topic of questions. What could be the reason for this? (In the traditional game, if a player is successful at removing a stick, that player goes again. However, for the sake of giving everyone more turns, I like to move on to the next player after each attempt is made.) If the black stick is successfully removed, the player should answer a question (I make these tough ones). Then she may use this black stick to help remove other sticks on her next turns. When the black stick is used or shared (I rarely see this - but it's another good processing point), a question from the "black" list should be answered. We love those dynamics!

Back to the rules. If another stick moves in the process of removing a stick, the player simply lets go of the stick she is touching, dropping it back onto the pile. Play until all the sticks are picked up, or until a sufficient amount of time goes by. I like to stop while it's still fun so my group will want to play again at another time.

> **Note:** I like to play this with small groups (4 - 5 players). I will provide a list of questions for every group (if I have enough players for more

than one group) to work from. I have found that sharing with a smaller group seems to be a bit less intimidating for some people. As I move through the small group activities, the players become more comfortable. When I think they're ready I can move into larger group sharing.

OBSERVATIONS/QUESTIONS:
- Has anyone ever played Pick-Up-Sticks® before?
- Was it an easy or difficult game? Did you think it was silly? Why?
- What skills are required to be successful at this game?
- What "color" questions did you like to answer the most?
- Was the black stick shared with other players? Why? Why not?
- Is it hard for you to talk in front of a group? Why do you think that is?
- Which questions did you try to avoid? Why?
- Did anyone have a question that you would have liked to answer? Would you like to answer that now?
- Did you learn anything about our group members?
- What would be a good category of questions to add if we were to play this again?

(others)
-
-

VARIATIONS:
- Provide a toothpick as a tool to assist in picking up sticks or straws.
- If you can, lay your hands on the "Handbook of Play Therapy," edited by Schaefer & O'Connor (1983). O'Connor has developed the Color-Your-Life technique that can be adapted to this activity.

OTHER IDEAS:
- If you want a book of questions all ready to go for you, pick up a copy of, "If anybody asks me..." by Larry Eckert, Wood-N-Barnes Publishing (see Recommended Resources). There are 1001 questions in 13 sections: You, Growing Up, Parents and Family, Friends and Peers, Relationships, Teen Angst, School, Sports, Past/Future, Perfection, Social Topics, On a Scale of 1-10, and What if... .

PICK YOUR BRAIN

RED - SELF IMAGE
*I have a high level of confidence in myself when it comes to... (p. 16)
*People seem to like me because... (p. 71)
*These are some things that I do "just for myself"... (p. 91)
*I would like to hold the world's record in... (p. 124)
*These are the nationalities I know are part of my heritage...and this is how I feel about that... (p. 140)
*The nicest compliment I ever received was... (p. 158)

GREEN - SOCIAL
*If I could create a holiday, it would be called...and this is how we would celebrate it... (p. 7)
*I tend to be a 'follower' rather than a 'leader' when... (p. 25)
*Someone I would really like to spend time with & learn from is... (p. 48)
*The most jealous I have ever been was when... (p. 49)
*This is how I feel about politics & politicians... (p. 318)
*The people I am most comfortable around are...because... (p. 348)

YELLOW - VALUES
*These are the characteristics that I think make the best leaders... (p. 36)
*The best gift I have received is... (p. 241)
*This is what I would die for... (p. 245)
*This is how money affects my family... (p. 268)
*I think a person is 'old' when... (p. 331)
*A time I put myself at risk to help others was... (p. 362)

BLUE - INTROSPECTION
*When other people cry, I... (p. 178)
*My favorite season of the year is... because... (p. 184)
*I hope I never have to... (p. 198)
*I have no patience when it comes to... (p. 224)
*My favorite work of art is... (p. 266)
*My dream career would be to... (p. 278)

BLACK - PERSONAL
*If I could change sexes for a day, I would... (p. 24)
*I have the biggest crush on... (from Chris)
*My last dream was about... (from Chris)

These questions come from a great journaling book - "The Me I See: Answering Life's Questions," by the Wood-N-Barnes Publishing Staff (see References).

TOSS-A-NAME GAME

Thanks to Karl Rohnke "Bottomless Bag Again."

NEEDS: A variety of throwable objects (stuffed animals to rubber chickens - also, check out how to make "Trash Balls" in Other Ideas). You also need some good overhead space and room for a good size circle.

PROCEDURE: Form a large circle with the group facing in. For round one, hand someone a soft throwable object and ask that player to hand off the object (not throw it) to the person to their left or right. As each person hands off the object, they say their own name. The object continues around the circle (in the initial hand off direction) until everyone has stated their name.

Play a second round. This time have the players toss (a "toss" being a nice soft throw) the object to anyone in the circle. Before the player tosses the object, have him state the person's name he is tossing it to (usually to someone they remember). Stating the name, we hope, will attract this person's attention. Then the toss is made. (Catching can be optional and used for "goal setting" purposes if this is where you want to go.) After the first object has been tossed around for a while, add another object to the circle, then another and another. Chaotic fun takes over and hopefully names are learned.

Note from Karl: Make sure that objects do not "ZING" across the circle. Nice tosses will ensure safety (I told you!). Stop while it's still fun and see who can state the names of all the group members.

Note from Chris: Keep a watchful eye on emotions and behaviors for this one - depending on your group. I have experienced some interesting "chaotic moments" that resulted in stopping the activity and discussing the situation so we could return to a more safe atmosphere.

OBSERVATIONS/QUESTIONS:
- Look around the circle. Do you know everyone's name?
- If you don't know a name, how can you find out what it is?
- What part of this game was easy? Why?
- When did the game get harder? Why was it hard?
- Did anyone toss an object without having the attention of the person you were tossing it to? Why did you toss it?
- Was catching the objects important? Why?
- What were some of the emotions during the game?
- Can anyone say the names of all the group members?
-
-

(others)

VARIATIONS:

·You can do this activity using other descriptors also (good with groups who already know each other). Favorite Color. What did you have for breakfast? Nickname. Middle Name. Favorite Food. Adventure Name (this is adding an adventure word to your first name using the first letter of your name, i.e., Crazy Chris).

OTHER **I**DEAS:

Move into "Messages" from this one.

Trash Balls: I have had lots of fun with these. I learned about Trash Balls from Bill Hazel (who said he learned from someone else). They can be used for many types of games - throwing, catching, and even kicking.

The process of making Trash Balls can be an activity in itself (or you can do them all yourself if you want, just be careful not to scratch your nose after working with newspaper). You'll need a whole bunch of newspaper, several rolls of masking tape, and lots of those plastic grocery bags (the medium-sized ones). (If you need bags try Wal-Mart; they give you about one bag for each item. FYI - these bags make great juggling scarves!!) So on we go.

Here's what you do. Have the group come together on the floor with all the stuff. Starting with the newspaper, wad up one sheet of paper at a time - not too tight. Tight wads end up being very heavy and not good to throw/toss at others. The idea is to wad one sheet, then get another sheet, wad it around the first, then get another sheet, wad it around the first two, etc. Keep going until you have created the size ball you want to use (keep it small enough to fit into the plastic bags you are using). Then loosely tape the newspaper wad together using the masking tape. (Working with another person makes this step easier - one person holds the wad, the other wraps the masking tape). **(Note:** If you pull too hard on the tape, it compacts the wad down and you lose the lightness of the ball. Put just enough tape around the wad to keep the shape - you'll be adding more.) Now tape the plastic bag around this semi-taped wad. The plastic bag helps keep the paper from ripping apart and keeps the black ink off everyone's fingers. I usually end up with about 50% of the plastic bag covered with masking tape. As the tape wears down, just slap some more on there. Or you could make a new one. (Please don't forget to recycle if you choose to throw the balls away!!)

If everybody in the group makes 1-2 trash balls, you'll have more than enough for a variety of games. I find that my groups get more involved with the games when they make the game balls themselves. Have fun!!

NAME BALL

Thanks to Frank Harris and Fearon Teacher Aids.

NEEDS: Two different colored lightweight balls and a mid-size open area. I like to use some spots for players to stand on - but they are not necessary.

PROCEDURE: Players stand in a circle, facing in, with space to permit catching and throwing a ball in any direction. This will be position "A." Each player learns the first name of the players on their left and right. Hand one of the players a ball. This lead player then names the person on his right and tosses the ball (henceforth designated as the "right ball") to that player. The ball is passed consecutively to the right, as each thrower names the person to whom he throws. The ball may be passed around the circle two or three times, so that players become familiar with each other's names. The facilitator then removes the "right ball" from the circle.

Using a different colored ball, a lead player tosses it to the player on his left, (henceforth the "left ball") saying this player's name. This ball is also passed consecutively to the left, as each thrower names the person to whom he is throwing. Again, the group can do this a few times around to get the names down. The facilitator then removes the "left ball" from the circle and hands the "right ball" back to any player.

Before the throwing starts again, players scramble around to different positions in the circle (not standing next to the same players they just left - or right!?). This is position "B." The player with the "right ball" locates the person who was on his right, names that person, and tosses the ball to that person. That player in turn does the same thing with the player who was on his right. Continue this tossing process. Should a player miss for any reason, that player or another player may pick the ball up and resume play, tossing to his "right" person.

When the passing is well along, add the "left ball." The first player with the ball finds the player that was on his left before the scrambling took place. Keep both balls going in their specified directions. Don't forget about name calling - not the bad kind either!

Once the game is well under way, additional "left" and "right" balls may be used. I try to stick with the same color for each direction, but that's me. Players can also be asked to change places more than once.

OBSERVATIONS/QUESTIONS:
- What was hard about the activity?
- What would have made the activity run smoother?

•Did anyone become confused during the game? How did you react?

•Is it okay to get confused? What makes it not okay?

•What might be the lesson learned here?

(others)

•

•

VARIATIONS:

•Add a rubber chicken to the circle. No one wants the rubber chicken so they are going to throw it to someone else - to anyone. What does the rubber chicken do to the process? What might you guess the rubber chicken stands for? What sorts of "rubber chickens" turn up in your life?

•How fast can the group return to position "A"? This is how I say it: "I'm going to time this next challenge. How fast can you return to position "A"? - GO!

OTHER **I**DEAS:

I'M GOING ON A TRIP

PROCEDURE: Ask the group to form a circle (I like to play this one hiking down a trail during backpack trips). Tell the group that you want them all to think of something to take on a trip. Appoint someone to go first. This player begins by saying their name and an item they want to take with them that begins with the same letter as their first name. For example, "My name is Mike, and I'm taking a melon on the trip." The next person, Bob, would say, "Mike is taking a melon. My name is Bob, and I'm taking a bat." The next player, John, would say, "Mike is taking a melon, Bob is taking a bat. My name is John, and I'm taking a joke." This continues around the circle until it gets back to Mike. I usually continue play with the first few players trying to say the entire groups' items - you don't want to let them out of the hard stuff!

If the players have difficulty remembering allow them extra time, or they may ask someone in the group for help. Discourage the group from helping until they are asked. Another great topic for discussion.

Talk with the group about how important it is not to laugh "at" but to laugh "with" others. Group members should be made aware of this early in your program so you can start the trust building right away. This is a good activity to emphasize this point and to support effort and risk.

OBSERVATIONS/QUESTIONS:
- How was this activity for you?
- Did anyone in the group say anything that made you uncomfortable?
- How did you react/feel when you forgot something?
- Is this a common reaction for you when you are uncomfortable?
- What would help you avoid such a reaction? How can others help?
- If you could go anywhere on a trip, where would you go?
- If you could take anyone on a trip with you, who would you take?
- What places have you traveled to so far?
- (others)
-

VARIATIONS:
- You could play this anytime using the alphabet in order.
- Continue around the circle one more time changing the items each person plans to take.

OTHER IDEAS:

NEEDS: Some fun things to say - there's a list below to get you started.

PROCEDURE: This grand old game is a great metaphor about the dangers of rumors and secrets. While sitting in a circle, one player in the group whispers a phrase, just once, into the ear of a person sitting next to them. That person whispers in the next player's ear just once, and so on around the circle until it travels back to the starter's ear. The starter tells the group what was heard, then tells them what was really said. I have yet to hear the final statement end up the same way it started.

Here are some ideas. Remember, the message does not have to be difficult. Try some easy ones first to see what happens.

1) Three tinkering tailors were terribly tired.
2) Samual Short's sister, Susie, sat sewing silently.
3) The banana bread breeze blew by the brother's bakery.
4) Two toads tried to hop across the wide road in search of a home.
5) Twenty tall Turks twirled their white tasseled turbans.
6) Six grown men raced across the river in their hiking boots.
7) Back in Boston the bakers of bread decided to put off baking.
8) Downtown Cleveland calls for cooler windy winter weather weekend.
9) Batman bought a basket of biscuits at the Gotham City bake sale.
10) What would happen if Wendy went to Washington on Wednesday?

OBSERVATIONS/QUESTIONS:
   •Was the message the same as when it started?
   •What do you think changed the message?
   •Who can tell me what a rumor is? Is it positive or negative?
   •Have you ever started a rumor?
   •Have you ever passed on a rumor? Why?
   •Have you ever been mentioned in a rumor that wasn't true? How did you feel about it? Were you able to correct it? How?
   •What is the best thing to do if you hear a rumor about someone?
(others) •
         •

VARIATIONS:

•Sit in a line (or a couple of lines) with every player facing one direction (each player is looking at the back of another player's head). Give the end person a simple picture - like the head of a cat, or a house with windows and doors. Have the end person, using his index finger, draw the picture on the back of the person in front of him. After the artwork is complete, have the next player do the same to the next person in line - and so on. The first person in line draws his idea of the back art on a piece of paper. Compare papers when finished. Take this a step farther. How would the picture turn out if everyone drew at the same time? (Only do this one if your group is comfortable with "touching.")

OTHER IDEAS:

NEEDS: A copy of the "Building My House" handout (see p. 25), and a pencil for each person.

PROCEDURE: I have the most success with this one when I do it in a relaxed setting - comfortable chairs or sitting on the floor. Give each person a handout and a pencil. Read the following questions to the group one at a time. Allow enough time for each person to write a response in the appropriate place on his or her sheet. It should be understood that they don't have to write a response if they would not be willing to share it with the group.

1) Along the foundation, write a value that governs your life.
2) Along the walls, write anything or anyone that supports you.
3) On the roof, write something that protects you.
4) By the television, write your favorite movie or TV show.
5) On the door, write something that you keep hidden from others.
6) In the chimney smoke, write a way that you blow off steam.
7) In the garden, write what you would plant if you could plant anything.
8) On the billboard, write what you are proud of and want others to see.
9) By the plane, write some place you would like to travel.
10) By the car, write what kind you would like to have.

Note: Be prepared, and allow enough time to answer questions about some of the terms you use. More than once I have had long discussions about what a "value" is.

Presenting this material can be done several ways. You could go around and share one question at a time or share them all at the end. With younger groups, I usually don't use all the questions at once. I'll come back to them over a period of time.

OBSERVATIONS/QUESTIONS:
- Did you learn something about yourself?
- Do you share any similar characteristics with anyone in the group?
- Was it hard for you to share personal things with the group?
- Did group members support your responses?
- What characteristics might change over time?
- What are some values that you might want to work toward?
- What are some constructive ways to blow off steam that were not mentioned? Were there some mentioned that you could try using?

(others)

• What will you want others to see in you five years from now?
•
•

VARIATIONS:

• Tape a blank piece of paper to either side of the handout and see what the group members want to add to the picture.

OTHER IDEAS:

BUILDING MY HOUSE

Name:_____

THOUGHTS · NOTES · REVELATIONS

SPOTTING

It will be important for you to read the following information on spotting if you intend to try Circle Pass on the next page.

Spotting is a term that means actively protecting the progress of another participant. A "human safety net" of sorts. The spotter's main purpose is to help prevent falls from causing injury. The spotter's primary duty is to protect the head and upper body of a participant using physical support.

A spotter does not hold up a participant, but is ready to protect if a fall occurs. Participants must realize that a spotter's duty is not to prevent a fall, it is to prevent injury. So, if both the spotter and participant end up on the ground without serious harm, the spotter has done his job.

There are 2 rules of correct spotting recommended by the Outdoor Institute of North Carolina (Wall, DeLano, & DeLano, 1991, p. 8):

1. Always pay **Attention.** The spotter must always watch the participant.
2. Fall **Anticipation.** The spotter is always ready with hands up.

The basic spotting position should be taught to all participants. This position can then be modified to fit the needs of each activity.

BASIC SPOTTING POSITION: The basic spot is arms up, slightly bent with hands open, one leg back from the other with foot turned out and knees slightly bent (see illustration). A spotter does not want to be rigid in the joints but rather absorbent so a participant is caught smoothly without being jolted to a stop.

CIRCLE PASS

Note: Please make sure to read the "Spotting" information on the previous page before attempting this activity.

NEEDS: A medium-size open area without obstacles.

PROCEDURE: Ask the group to form a shoulder-to-shoulder circle, facing in. For this activity I like to be the first person to demonstrate. This will establish the level of ability and give others a chance to see how it is done, risk-free (unless they drop me, then I have to process before trying again).

I become the Active Participant (AP), standing in the middle of the circle with my hands crossed over my chest (hopefully having nothing to do with being dead!). The members of the circle will be spotting, using the basic position (see Spotting, p. 27). As the center person, staying as rigid as possible (stiff as a board), I fall back into the circle. The spotters will then, carefully **without shoving**, pass me around the circle.

It will be very important for the AP to stay inflexible and straight at all times, keeping feet together and planted on the ground as if they were glued to a board. It might even be helpful to have a spotter hold down the AP's feet as the passing is going on.

After a few passes, encourage the AP to close her eyes. Spotters should absorb the weight of the AP and let her have a comfortable experience. When the AP is ready to stop (or you as the facilitator feel it's time to change) she should say, "hands on." At this point all the spotters put both hands on the AP until she is steady and upright in the middle of the group (this is a really cool feeling). When the AP has her bearings she can then change positions with someone who is ready to try. Give each group member a chance to be in the middle. It will be very important to watch the spotting carefully during each passing.

Don't forget about challenge by choice. Group members do not have to go into the middle. There may be some major trust issues still unresolved for some people. Maybe something they saw when others were in the middle lowered their trust. These are all great things to talk about with your group. If each person is at least willing to spot, then they are working toward trusting each other. If someone is sitting out, then you might want to reconsider this activity until everyone is willing to support the group.

OBSERVATIONS/**Q**UESTIONS:
- What was it like to be in the center? Was it different with your eyes closed?
- Did you trust everyone in the circle? Why? Why not?
- Do you consider yourself a trusting person? What builds trust for you?
- Was there any point when you were nervous? What happened?
- Were the participants in the middle able to keep their body straight?
- What was it like to have all those hands on you?
- What would you say about the trust level of an AP who bends at the waist? What prevents them from keeping their body straight?
- How can we help participants be more trusting?
- What are the feelings of participants who did not take a turn?
- Is it okay not to take a turn?
-
-

(others)

VARIATIONS:
There is a second part that I like to add with groups that are really working well together. After each person in the group has had a chance to be in the middle, ask if there is anyone who would like to go again and then be lifted up into the air. I'm part of the circle this time, so I can demonstrate what the lead person will do.

After conducting the circle pass again (really try to encourage the AP to close their eyes for this one), I ask the AP to turn their back to me. I place one of my hands on the AP's neck and one on the back of his head. Keeping his body stiff (very important - DON'T SIT DOWN), the AP leans back toward me. As this is happening, the other members of the circle place their hands under the AP's back and legs, slowly lifting and holding the AP at the groups' waist level. (The lead participant's responsibility at all times is to protect the head and neck of the AP. The lead also calls all the lifting motions.) I ask the AP, "Do you want to go higher?" If so, I count, "One, two, ready, lift." The group raises the AP to their shoulder level. I ask again, "Do you want to go higher?" If the answer is yes, I ask the AP to open his eyes for this last lift, then I count again. The group may only lift to the height of the maximum reach of the shortest person in the group. Then we reverse the process, step by step, to set him back down. (Setting the AP down also happens any time he or she does not want to go higher.) Make sure the feet are set down first and then carefully - all together - set the person into an upright, standing position. Don't let go until you are sure the person is ready to stand on their own!

After I demo the first round, I let the AP choose the lead for the lift. It is good to observe who is chosen. (Always monitor the lead person.) This activity is meant to increase the trust level within the group. Remember, everyone does not have to participate!

Note: This activity takes at least 30 minutes. (I just had to add it.)

OTHER **I**DEAS:

NEEDS: 2 blindfolds, 2 bell-balls (balls with bells in them [cat toy] or film containers with BBs inside), and an open area for a large circle.

PROCEDURE: Form a large-size circle in an open area. Choose 2 volunteers who are willing to be blindfolded. From the 2, pick a tagger and a taggee. Put the blindfolds on. The leader moves each person into the circle somewhere, then carefully hands each a bell-ball without giving away the other person's position.

The tagger must find and tag the other person. The tagger is allowed 3 separate rings with the ball. The taggee must answer with a ring each time. The taggee can ring as many times as he/she wishes. The tagger must answer each time. The rest of the group acts as silent bumpers to prevent the 2 players from leaving the circle. Silence is very important in this game (and often the hardest part of the process). When the tagger finally tags the taggee or his/her 3 rings are used up without tagging, switch rolls to give the taggee a chance to be a tagger. The round is over after a tag or 3 rings. Choose 2 other players. Play enough times to give everyone a chance to play both roles.

OBSERVATIONS/QUESTIONS:
   • What was it like being blindfolded?
   • What quality does it take to be blindfolded in front of other people?
   • What was it like to be the tagger? Did you have a plan?
   • What was it like to be the taggee? Did you have a strategy?
   • What role did the rest of the group have?
   • Did everyone in the group follow directions?
   • What happens when people don't follow directions?
   • Could you share your level of trust with group members?
   • What types of things bring down trust levels?
   •
   •

(others)

VARIATIONS:

- Only blindfold the tagger. When the tagger rings, the sighted taggee has 3 seconds to answer (3 seconds to move around in the circle). When the taggee answers the ring - with a ring - she must stay still until the tagger either tags her or rings the bell-ball again.
- Play outside in a leafy area without the bell-balls. It will be important to have very quiet circle protectors for this one.
- For smaller groups, I like to play this way. Have a blindfolded player sit "Indian style" in the center of a large circle of players. Place the bell-ball 1' in front of the blindfolded player - I'll shake it before I put it down. Then pick someone to try and get the ball without being touched by the blind folded player. The blindfolded player can only move his arms to tag a sighted stealer - he is not allowed to get up. If the ball is successfully taken, have the stealer be the new protector. This is a great one outside in the leaves!

ADDITIONAL IDEAS:

FIREBALL

Thanks to Brian Brolin.

This is an adaptation of a traditional "Honor" game played by some American Indian tribes. They often played games like **Fireball** and **Flinch** (see p. 35) to teach teamwork and honor.

NEEDS: One small throwable object (an authentic fireball if you can find one - contact Brian), and a medium-size area.

PROCEDURE: Players form a large circle and toss the ball to each other following these rules:

1) Players cannot speak.
2) Players are not allowed to move except to catch or throw the ball.
3) Players cannot make a bad throw or catch.

After a few games add this rule:

4) If the leader points at a player, that player must kneel down.

Do not define the rules for the players. If they ask, just say, "It is up to you and only you." Observe how rules are interpreted. If a rule is broken, the player must step back from the circle and kneel down on one knee. The game continues until only 2 or 3 players remain. Stress the point that it is the individual's choice to kneel down, being a test of honesty and honor within themselves.

A friend of mine likes to present the game this way: "This is a game of honor. Honor is not easy to achieve. It is held in the minds of others about you, from watching what you do. In this game a fact is a fact; a bad throw is a bad throw; a bad catch is a bad catch; a noise is a noise. Others will see this and judge you for your choices. Their interpretation may be more important than yours. In the end, however, you must decide!" (Something of this nature.)

OBSERVATIONS/QUESTIONS:
- Why did you kneel down?
- If you knelt down, did you lose?
- Should someone have knelt down who didn't? What did you do?
- To whom does the choice belong?
- What were individual definitions of the rules?
- What is at stake if people stretch or break the rules?
- What sort of reputation might that person obtain?

•Is it easy to change a reputation? What would it take?
•What is "Honor"?
•How do you obtain honor?
•Why is honor important?
•Is there anyone you know who possesses honor?
•How did you feel/react when the leader pointed at you to kneel?
•Why do you think the leader pointed at you?

(others)
•
•

(See **Flinch** questions on the next page.)

OTHER **I**DEAS:

FLINCH

Thanks to Brian Brolin.

NEEDS: One small throwable object (a fireball if you have one - contact Brian if interested), and a medium-size area to play.

PROCEDURE: Form a large circle with the leader in the center. Players stand perfectly still with arms crossed in front of them facing the leader. Give these rules:

1) Players cannot move except to catch and throw the object.
2) Players cannot make any sounds during the game.

The leader tosses the object randomly at players. Be sure to turn around enough to interact with everyone. Players must catch the object, throw it back to the leader, and then recross their arms. The leader can fake a toss to a player also. If the player moves or makes a sound when there has been no throw, he or she must back out of the circle and kneel down on one knee. The game continues until only 2 or 3 players are left standing.

Just as in **Fireball**, players are ultimately responsible for themselves. **Flinch** is a game that can build honor and trust.

OBSERVATIONS/QUESTIONS:
- Was it hard to play this game? What made it hard?
- What reason did you have for kneeling?
- Did anyone influence your decision to kneel?
- What was some of the self-talk in your head during the game? Where do you think self-talk comes from?
- What is important about following directions?
- What kind of person follows directions? What kind of person doesn't?
- What kind of person do you want to be seen as? Why?
- Are other people's opinions important to you? Why?
-
-

(others)

(See **Fireball** questions.)

VARIATIONS:
- I like to play a non-elimination type game. If a player breaks a rule the first time, place hands on hips; the second time, hands on head; the third time, hands on knees. If any player reaches the third phase, I usually start a new game with one of the players becoming the leader. Then I take a spot in the circle.
- With a small group, have the players line up in front of the leader in a semi-circle shape.

OTHER **I**DEAS:

NEEDS: Three tossable objects, and an area for a medium-size circle.

Note: This is my variation on the classic "Group Juggling."

PROCEDURE: Form a medium-size circle facing in. Include yourself in the circle as the leader (at first). Take one message (a tossable object) and create a pattern within the circle by throwing it (nicely) to someone across from you. Continue the throws until everyone has received the message only once and thrown it only once. You, as the leader, should make the first and receive the last throw. I like to ask each person in the group to cross their arms in front of their body after they have caught and tossed the object. This way the tosser can find the uncrossed tossees easier.

Once a pattern is established, try it again with one object to confirm that everyone remembers who they throw to and catch from. Once this skill is mastered, add another message (object) to the pattern. Toss one after the other. See if the group can get both around. You can start to do some goal setting; for example: How many drops will we allow ourselves? Let's not drop any messages. How fast can we get them around?, etc. Add a third message to the conversation and so on until the group finds its maximum potential. I have had a few groups that could get around one object apiece - everyone in the group must throw their object at the same time!

OBSERVATIONS/**Q**UESTIONS:
- What were players doing to make the activity easier?
- What problems were occurring?
- What suggestions could you make to help solve the problem(s)?
- Which solution could we try?
- What happens when we send a message to someone who isn't ready?
- What are some ways we can tell someone is ready for a message?
- How can you prevent messages from colliding?
- What did you feel like when you dropped a message?
- Did the other players say anything?
- How do negative comments affect performance?
- How do positive and supportive comments affect performance?
-
-

(others)

VARIATIONS:

•**Timing** this activity can be a great problem solving challenge. Stick with just timing 3 messages around the pattern with these two rules: 1) You must stick to the same pattern, and 2) Each player must touch all 3 objects. Have someone in the group help time from start to finish (someone in the middle of the pattern. Or, if you started this activity without playing, then you can time it.) After the first round of passing 3 objects, ask the group if they can get a faster time. Ask what changes they need to make to get that faster time. Most groups will stay in the same circle they started in and just move in closer or just "throw faster." Challenge them to think laterally. Whatever time they achieve, cut it in half. Tell them you know they are a high functioning group and they can do it. It is possible to get under 5 seconds with a group of 12. Don't give out any answers, be strong. Come back to the activity another time if they don't discover they can change standing positions and stand next to the person they are throwing it to. Always try to end with a successful round, then move on.

Karl Rohnke has some good ones:
•Call out "Reverse" half way through the sequence.
•Start 2 objects in one direction and 2 in the other direction.
•Add an object as a "rumor" which can go anywhere. What are the effects of rumors in our communication process? A friend of mine uses one of those rubber chickens as a rumor, then asks about the "rubber chickens" that present themselves in our lives.
•On a hot day use water balloons.

OTHER **I**DEAS:

NEEDS: You will want to prepare at least 2 separate puzzles with enough pieces for each person in the group to have at least 1 piece. I use the large panels of 2 <u>identical</u> cereal boxes (you will see why in a second). If you want, cut the pictures in crazy puzzle shapes. Be careful to keep the 2 pictures' pieces separate (for now). I have used a paper cutter to cut angled shapes and it works out just great. (Don't rule out the 12-piece puzzles with the big pieces made for younger kids that you can find at most toy stores.)

PROCEDURE: Place 1 dismantled puzzle in a box or bag and bring it to the group. Conceal a few of the second puzzle's pieces in your pocket for later. Present the boxed puzzle pieces to the group. Have each person remove 1 piece until all are gone. Tell the group you will time them to see how long it takes to put the puzzle together; each group member adding his/her own puzzle piece to the final picture.

Make another attempt to see if the group can better their time. Usually the group will want to try again. On a third attempt, I "secretly" trade the pieces in my pocket for some in the box (you've got to be sneaky - you don't want to get caught or the lesson may be lost). Then start them off. <u>Be ready</u> for anything here. I have experienced everything from anger to laughter depending on the population. Process the reactions.

OBSERVATIONS/**Q**UESTIONS:
  - Describe what the activity was like for you?
  - What sorts of communication did you use?..or not use?
  - What made the activity easy? What if the picture wasn't clear? Do we always have a clear picture of what things will be like?
  - Did anyone "hold out" their piece so they could be the last to play? What might be the reason for doing this?
  - What reactions took place when the mismatched pieces were added?
  - Is this your common reaction to change?
  - Can you completely stop change from happening?
  - What can you do to "change" your reaction to change?
  - Do you want to try the activity again with the proper pieces?..or 2 puzzles?

(others)
  -
  -

VARIATIONS:

•Clifford Knapp (1988) uses a large leaf, the single blade kind (not the compound kind). Tear the leaf up into pieces and follow the procedure above. Mr. Knapp also likes to do the activity without verbal communication.

OTHER **I**DEAS:

STICKS, STONES & BONES

Adapted from Knapp's "Communication Patterns" activity.

NEEDS: For each pair of group members you will need 2 matching colored popsicle sticks (Sticks), 2 similar small rocks or dice (Stones), 2 matching dominos (Bones), and an indoor or outdoor area where it is comfortable to sit down. You can also use any items as long as each player in the pair of players has matching objects (if you read on it will make more sense).

PROCEDURE: The only preparation part that takes a little time is coloring the sticks (I have some youth help me the night before - using markers). Make sure that every 2 sticks have the same colored patterns on them; all the sticks in the group do not have to match.

This is a good activity for understanding directions and how they can be misunderstood. When you're ready, creatively pair up group members (if you use popcicle sticks, give each player a stick and have them find their match). Give each player in the pair half of a matching set of the above gear: 1 Stick, 1 Stone, and 1 Bone. Have the partners sit back-to-back on the ground or floor. Have each pair decide who will be the leader for the first round. The leader starts by arranging the 3 items in a pattern on the ground in front of him/herself, and then attempts to describe the arrangement to his/her partner. The partner is not allowed to speak or look around during the activity. When completed, have the partners look at each other's patterns. (If you think it is needed, ask a few questions, but don't completely process until after each player has been a leader.) Switch roles and repeat the activity. I like to time this activity to keep transitions consistent.

OBSERVATIONS/QUESTIONS:
- How did you do?
- Did the patterns turn out the same? Why or why not?
- How did leaders feel when they saw their partner's patterns?
- Where did problems arise between the two of you?
- Did you and your partner figure out a way to communicate nonverbally?
- Was it easy to follow the rules of the task?
- What would the task have been like if you could have asked questions?
- Would asking questions help you do a better job?
- How would asking questions help the leader do a better job?
- What is important about questions?
- What tends to happen if we don't ask questions when we're confused?
-
-

(others)

41

VARIATIONS:
- •If there is time, repeat the activity and allow partners to talk.
- •Add more matching objects.
- •Give each person 5-6 building blocks. Have the leader build and describe a sculpture.
- •A fun variation is to buy some of those small lego block sets - like a car or a bug (something with less than 50 pieces). Then give one partner the box and the other the parts. Sit back-to-back and let them talk but not look at what the other has. Can they create what is on the box?

OTHER **I**DEAS:

CAVE IN

Thanks to Jim Cain & Barry Jolliff.

NEEDS: Bring in a large tablecloth or blanket that can completely cover the group. Be sure to use a material that is an open weave and allows air movement. Plastic material is not a good choice. If you can have darkness in your room, bring one small flashlight also.

Note: Cave In can be an emotionally intense experience. This activity is intended for groups that have a long-term relationship and have intimate knowledge and respect for each other.

PROCEDURE: The challenge is for the participants to take part in a simulated cave-in, where only one member of the group is guaranteed survival. The group must collectively decide which member of the group is the best choice to leave and seek rescue assistance, knowing that the fate of the group members are uncertain.

When the group is ready (turn out lights if you can) get under the blanket in close quarters. A tight circle usually works the best. Then tell the group, "The cavern we were exploring has suddenly flooded, causing the massive walls to collapse. The situation is extremely dangerous. Only a portion of the original opening to the cavern is still passable. Only one light was saved from the flooding. If only two of us can be assured a safe exit, which one person from the group will go with me for help?" (I tell them I have to go so that the authorities will believe our story.)

In the discussion encourage decisions to be made based on logical processing, but take into account the emotional comments as well. Only choose the one person to escape safely. Ranking the remaining group members is unnecessary (it can have the same effect as being chosen last for a baseball game).

When the one person is chosen, we leave the covered setting and ask the remainder of the group to stay behind. I like to observe the group for a few minutes to see and hear what takes place. This is even more dynamic when the room is dark and they are left without light. Then, as Jim suggests, "It is essential, when completing this activity, to simulate a complete rescue of ALL group members from the survival situation. This reinforces that no matter what the priority of the group member chosen to leave, all the participants have value and are worthy of rescue."

One last suggestion. This activity can be very draining and may leave the group in a less than positive mood. Try and add some positive energy for everyone before they go. Put together some fun "Are you more like...." (see p. 97) choices so they have a chance to share some positive traits with each other.

OBSERVATIONS/QUESTIONS:

- Now that the activity is over, what are your feelings about it?
- Can you recall and share some of the feelings you were experiencing during the activity?
- What did you observe about the decision making process?
- For those that remained behind, were you comfortable with the group decision?
- What quality seemed to be the major influence on the final decision?
- How is this quality similar to what our society values?..our group values?
- Are there any qualities or behaviors less accepted than others? Why do you think this happens? Who decides what is acceptable?
- Is there really a best choice for this simulation, or given the right set of circumstances, could anyone be acceptable?
- Did you learn anything new about any members of the group?
- Have you ever had to make a very difficult decision before? Would you be willing to share it with the group?

(others)
-
-

VARIATIONS:

- In the book "Values Clarification," by Simon, Howe, & Kirschenbaum, there is another variation of **Cave In**. They ask each group member 2 questions and then rank from first out to last out. The first out have a better chance of survival. 1) What do you have to live for? 2) What do you have to contribute to others if you survive? (If you don't have a copy of this book yet, I highly recommend it!)

OTHER IDEAS:

COLOR CHALLENGE

Thanks to William M. Hazel.

NEEDS: You will need a copy of the blank "Color Challenge Grid" and the 16 "Color Challenge Markers" (see pgs. 47-48). Color the markers if you can for added visual effect - or not, the really hard version - then cut the markers out before you start. There should be 4 Squirrels (Blues), 3 Lizards (Yellows), 3 Frogs (Reds), 3 Turtles (Greens), and 3 Snakes (Whites).

PROCEDURE: The objective of this initiative is to have the group place all of the markers, one for each square, on the squares using the following guidelines.

1. No two markers of the same animal/color should be in line vertically.
2. No two markers of the same animal/color should be in line horizontally.
3. No two markers of the same animal/color should be in line diagonally.

Ask the group to place the markers, 4 at a time, covering a row (horizontal line). Establish that all players in the group must be in complete agreement before placing the markers on the grid. The group is allowed to go back and change any row (not a column - vertical) at any time, as long as every group member agrees to the change.

As the facilitator, you may add some limits on changes or allow the group to have any number of changes they need. The important aspect here is that everyone should stay involved in the process.

Mr. Hazel suggests, "Use this initiative only with a group that has already achieved a certain degree of social comfort. Agreeing on the layout of each row may lead to lots of conflict and frustration. Remember that the developmental objective is to allow the group to work through this process. What happens during the activity is what's important, not if the group is able to solve the problem. Be sure to make this distinction before you begin."

OBSERVATIONS/**Q**UESTIONS:
- Did anyone take on a leadership role during the activity?
- Would anyone be willing to give feedback on the leadership style(s) that emerged in the group?
- What is important about leadership?
- How did the group decide to communicate? Did the group follow up on this plan or did it change?
- Did anyone feel that they were not heard? Did you do anything about it?
- Is "complete agreement" always the best way? When is it good to use and when might it not be so good?

•What was it like for you to have a voice in the decision making process?

•How do you react/behave when you don't have a say?

•Do you think you should always have a say in things that affect your life? When shouldn't you have a say?

•How did you gauge your success? Was it all or nothing? Batting 75% is a fantastic average in baseball.

(others)

•

•

VARIATIONS:

•Use different markers like money, numbers, balls, cookies, shoes, furniture... stuff like that.

•For a larger version that everyone can stand around, place a 4 x 4 grid on the floor using blank sheets of white paper. You could use colored construction paper to cover the spots.

•To make the activity a bit easier (then progress to the harder), take out the diagonal rule.

OTHER IDEAS:

(You don't have to look anymore for the answer because I didn't put it in here. Now you can play the first time. How will your opinion affect the process of the group? Boy, that doesn't happen very much, does it?!)

COLOR CHALLENGE GRID

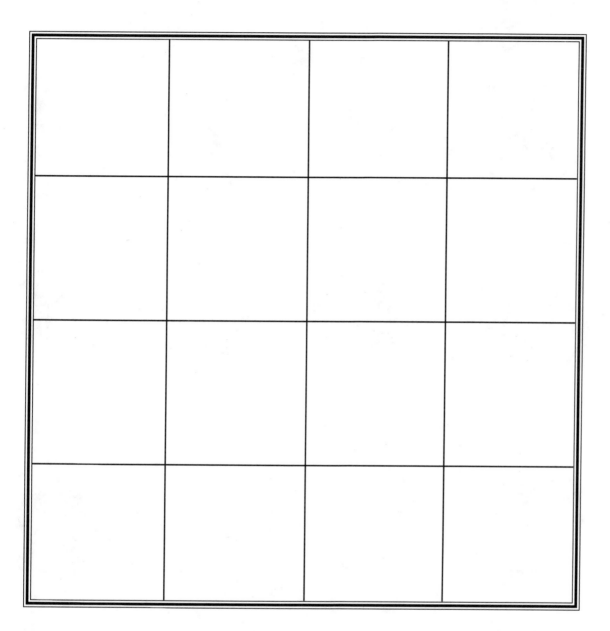

Place all of the markers, covering one horizontal row at a time, on the squares using the following guidelines:

    1. No two markers of the same animal/color should be lined up vertically.
    2. No two markers of the same animal/color should be lined up horizontally.
    3. No two markers of the same animal/color should be lined up diagonally.

COLOR CHALLENGE MARKERS

PAPER CHUTE

Thanks to Sam Sikes, Executive Marbles

NEEDS: I like to work in pairs for this one, so I provide four 8 1/2" x 11" pieces of paper and 6 paper clips for each set of pairs (can you have a set of pairs?). You will also need a stopwatch.

PROCEDURE: After cleverly dividing your group into couples, give them their resources. Ask each pair to construct an apparatus using all of the resources provided that, when dropped from 8', will take the longest possible time to reach the floor.

In layman's terms, make something that will take the longest to float down to the ground - using all the resources. Easy one.

I tend to set a time limit on this to force on-task behaviors - 5 minutes usually works very well. When the building time is over, the groups have to gather at the drop zone. No more building or adaptations can take place in the drop zone area. To reach the 8' dropping height, someone in the group will have to stand on top of something - this something should be very stable. I hope I don't need to give a long description of the safety that needs to be considered?! Please be careful! I will time the drops from when the chute is let go until it hits the ground. Be careful not to stop the watch too soon. Sometimes the chutes catch an up-draft at the end.

During the construction phase of this activity, be sure to walk around observing group interactions so that you can generate some processing topics.

OBSERVATIONS/QUESTIONS:
- What did you find to be the most difficult part of this activity?
- Did you and your partner put any planning into your chute or did you just start to build?
- Which one of you took on the leadership role? How did it help or hinder the process?
- Were each of you able to share ideas with the other? Whose idea ended up as the final product? Did you use any of the other groups' ideas? Why? Is this okay to do?
- Was it easy to work with your partner? What made it easy? What made it hard?
- How did your chute float? How would you change it to make it float longer? Where did you get this new idea?
- How did the group react to each pairs' chute? Positive? Negative? Encouraging? Sympathetic? Supportive?

•What one resource would you add to this activity to make it more successful for you?

•

•

VARIATIONS:

•Give each pair 8 super-size drinking straws, 30 inches of masking tape and a raw egg. Ask each pair to create a protective structure for the egg so when it is dropped from eight feet it will not crack. The infamous EGG DROP.

OTHER **I**DEAS:

NEEDS: A box and whatever you want to put inside of it. A piece of paper and a pencil for each group member. (I have a shoe box filled with strategy puzzle games that I like to play after this one. Any time I can work on problem solving I will gladly take. Beside, kids really like the puzzles. A great source of these types of games is the MindWare catalog. See p. 83 in the **Minute Mysteries** section for details.)

PROCEDURE: This was one of those spur-of-the-moment activities I came up with because I didn't have time to play with the puzzles and it wasn't time to go yet. Plus, everyone kept asking me, "What's in the box?" I finally said, "What do you think is in the box?" And so the monster was born.

The Box activity has turned out to be an interesting indicator of some creative thought processes within my group. There has been an interesting correlation between the length of one's list and their willingness to participate in group activities and discussions. Clues lead us to the treasure!

So choose a box, any size of box. A refrigerator box is likely to produce a much longer list than a ring box. Then decide what to put in the box. Some snacks might be fun. You could bring an empty box, but every group guesses that one.

OBSERVATIONS/**Q**UESTIONS:
- What sorts of lists were compiled? Foods? Clothing items? Weapons? Childlike items? Adultish items? A mix?
- What does this activity remind you of?
- Did anyone in the group guess correctly? Did it matter?
- Who was able to think of a lot of different items? Who was able to think of just a few? Is this okay?
- Why do you think I asked you to participate in this activity?
- Were you disappointed when you found out what was inside?
- How is anticipation different from reality? Is this good or bad?
- What other times have you anticipated something only to be disappointed?
- Could there be a good lesson to learn from this activity? What?
-
-

(others)

OTHER **I**DEAS:

SECTION TWO

What would it be like...?

THOUGHTS · NOTES · REVELATIONS

What would it be like to have a whole bunch of questions that started with, "What would it be like...?" You're not sure? Well, here is your chance to find out. The list that follows can be integrated into transition time, group session, or bus trips. Anytime really.

The following questions are presented in closed format. This means they can be answered with one word (usually a feeling word in this case). It is your choice as a facilitator to expand on the questions if you think the individual is ready to do so and you have the time. Sometimes it is better to let one word answers be enough. This can build trust for future discussions.

If you choose to work with one word feeling answers, you could provide a copy of "EMOTIONS" (found at the end of this section, p. 63). Encourage the group members to be creative using answers from the sheet. Then maybe you could even expand on the feeling word (a great way to practice the use of a dictionary). You just never know what can happen.

If you would like to expand on the questions, here's the idea: "What would it be like to move to a new state?" Answers could vary from scary to great (it would get me out of here!). Expanding on the responses is also wide open. "What sorts of things would be scary?" "Why do you want to get out of here?" Then expand upon those answers. You get the idea.

I have presented these questions a couple of ways. I've just opened the book and said, "Who would like to pick a number?" This makes the atmosphere relaxed and non-threatening. Other times I planned ahead and picked questions that related to a certain group discussion that I wanted to have. Both ways have worked well.

Be careful not to spend too much time with one person. I always allow the option to pass or choose a new question. (I usually don't allow more than one chance to pick another question - time problems). If the question seems to cause reactions with others, open the question up to the group. (I usually set up guidelines to prevent others from answering someone else's question or blurting out an answer.) Use your time evenly among the group members to keep the interest going.

Don't forget to take a turn yourself. It is a good way to become part of the group. Have fun with the questions so you'll leave them wanting more! Also, I have to plug another great resource. If you like the "question" type format, check out "The Me I See: Answering Life's Questions," by Wood & Barnes Publishing Staff. It's a journaling book with 400 questions in it (see references).

Have fun! And if your group wants to make up more questions, send them to the publisher for inclusion in the next **Games (& other stuff) for Group**!!

WHAT WOULD IT BE LIKE...

1. if you were President of the United States?
2. to go to summer camp?
3. to fly to the moon?
4. to go ahead into the future?
5. to hike for a week in the desert?
6. to move to a new state?
7. if you couldn't see?
8. to own your own island?
9. if you had to fight in a war?
10. to go dog sledding?
11. if you were lost in a cave by yourself?
12. to be in a musical band?
13. if you couldn't walk?
14. to be invisible?
15. if you discovered a cure for cancer?
16. to stay in a hospital overnight?
17. to rescue a cat from a tree?
18. if you couldn't use your hands?
19. to go back in time?
20. to swim with a dolphin?
21. if you couldn't speak?
22. to write a book?
23. to discover a new land?
24. if you couldn't hear?
25. to spend the day with _____? (pick person of interest)
26. to go bungee jumping?
27. if we all looked the same?
28. to live in space?
29. to live on a different planet?
30. going over a waterfall in a barrel?
31. to drive a race car?
32. if you were pulled over by a police officer?
33. to change your name?
34. to live in a log cabin?

WHAT WOULD IT BE LIKE...

35. to witness a car accident?

36. to mud wrestle?

37. to go to a boarding school?

38. to drive on the left side of the road?

39. to be the ruler of a small country?

40. to fly on a magic carpet?

41. to be a bus driver?

42. to forget your wallet on a dinner date?

43. to live in an underwater city?

44. to climb the stairs of the Statue of Liberty?

45. to be the opposite gender?

46. to be snowbound in a tent?

47. to drive an eighteen wheeler across the United States?

48. if you hit an animal that was crossing the road?

49. if your parents broke a promise?

50. to be the boss of a large company?

51. to be a performer in a traveling circus?

52. not to have a home to live in?

53. to be in a dance troupe that performed around the world?

54. if someone said you were stupid?

55. to fly a plane?

56. if you could trade places with your teacher?

57. to die your hair orange?

58. to have your own car?

59. if you were a movie star?

60. to have a paper route?

61. to be on television?

62. to live with a different family?

63. to have a new sister?

64. to have a new brother?

65. to have your own children?

66. to travel in a time machine?

67. to work in a toy factory?

68. if there were no school?

WHAT WOULD IT BE LIKE...

69. to go to Disneyland?

70. if you told your best friend's secret to someone else?

71. to have a million dollars?

72. to be the pitcher on a major league baseball team?

73. to be a bird?

74. to be in a parade?

75. to look out over Paris from the Eiffel tower?

76. if you woke up to find your skin a different color?

77. to be a mountain lion?

78. if everyone you knew forgot your birthday?

79. to be the quarterback on a football team?

80. to receive a puppy?

81. to go anywhere that you want?

82. to be the only one home, and someone was trying to break in?

83. to meet a king?

84. to choose your own chores?

85. to teach an adult something you were very good at?

86. to be a fish?

87. to stay out as long as you wanted?

88. to have a secret hideout?

89. to be all by yourself for a day?

90. to be all by yourself for a week?

91. to lie to your best friend?

92. without television?

93. to travel cross country on a train?

94. to be in the Olympics?

95. without cars?

96. parachuting out of a plane?

97. to fall in the mud with your best clothes on?

98. to be on probation--someone following your every move?

99. to speak in front of a large group?

100. to be a teacher's favorite student?

101. to wake up and be an adult?

WHAT WOULD IT BE LIKE...

102. to work in a factory?

103. to sail around the world?

104. to travel in a blimp?

105. to stay overnight in jail?

106. to find $10?

107. to find $1000?

108. to meet the President of the United States?

109. to be a doctor of medicine?

110. to have an identical twin?

111. to have your own house?

112. to have your own horse?

113. to work on a farm?

114. to have the ability to see into the future?

115. to find out that you were adopted?

116. to live in the mountains?

117. to lose all your hair?

118. to go SCUBA diving?

119. to wear a uniform to school?

120. to go to a Six Flags amusement park?

121. to never have to clean your room?

122. to ride across America on a bike?

123. to pick a nickname for yourself?

124. to be a police officer?

125. to be a dog?

126. to be the principal of your school?

127. to trade lives with someone else?

128. to ride in a hot air balloon?

129. to clean the windows of a skyscraper?

130. to find a buried treasure?

131. to change your parents?

132. to share something you are proud of?

133. being stranded at sea in a life raft?

134. to be a fire fighter?

WHAT WOULD IT BE LIKE...

135. to have rich parents?

136. to have private use of an amusement park for a day?

137. to be without gravity?

138. to live on a planet where it rained every day?

139. if you didn't own shoes?

140. to live on a different planet?

141. to run out of gas on a date?

142. to live in a cave?

143. to win an Olympic medal?

144. to lose everything you owned in a fire?

145. to ride in the space shuttle?

146. to be a cheerleader?

147. to save someone who was drowning?

148. to win a Nobel Prize?

149. to sleep the night in a graveyard?

150. to skin a deer?

151. to own your own business?

152. to own a professional sports team?

153. to make the winning shot in a basketball game?

154. to miss the winning shot in a basketball game?

155. to build a house with no power tools?

156. to save someone who was choking?

157. to say something nice about yourself?

158. to be a hero?

159. to perform on Broadway?

160. to go to a one-room school?

161. to change one thing about the way you look?

162. to cheat on a test?

163. to have bad acne?

164. to wear hand-me-down clothes?

165. to get rid of your biggest fear?

166. to be confined indoors for 6 months?

167. to find out you had a terminal illness?

WHAT WOULD IT BE LIKE...

168. to find out your best friend had a terminal illness?

169. to share your room with another person?

170. to get caught in a thunderstorm?

171. to experience an earthquake?

172. to go to school all year long?

173. to choose any job you wanted?

174. to be granted just one wish (no asking for more wishes)?

175. to eat the same food every day for a week?

176. to find a stray dog?

177. to change a baby's diaper?

178. to have a disabled brother or sister?

179. to drive a motorcycle?

180. to live in Alaska?

181. to be a famous musician?

182. to be a foreign exchange student?

183. if the world ran out of gas?

184. to marry a prince or princess?

185. to have no rules?

186. to do one thing you are not allowed to do?

187. if you could join any group?

188. to have your own holiday?

189. to have a street named after you?

190. if you gave away everything you owned?

191. to be stranded on a desert island?

192. to have a scary dream?

193. to be an only child?

194. to go ski jumping?

195. to ride in a bobsled?

196. to make your own laws?

197. to give up one of your kidneys to save a life?

198. to give blood?

199. if the drinking age changed to 25?

200. to be voted the most attractive person alive?

WHAT WOULD IT BE LIKE...

201. to have one magical power?
202. to never be teased again for anything?
203. to be extremely overweight?
204. to grow all the food you had to eat?

Add your own:

Add your own...Submit your ideas of more "What would it be like..." for a future publication to:
Mony Cunningham, Wood 'N' Barnes Publishing, 2717 NW 50th, OKC, OK 73112

WHAT WOULD IT BE LIKE...

Add your own...Submit your ideas of more "What would it be like..." for a future publication to:
Mony Cunningham, Wood 'N' Barnes Publishing, 2717 NW 50th, OKC, OK 73112

eMotiONs©

aggressive	alienated	angry	annoyed	anxious	apathetic	bashful
bored	cautious	confident	confused	curious	depressed	determined
disappointed	discouraged	disgusted	embarrassed	enthusiastic	envious	ecstatic
excited	exhausted	fearful	frightened	frustrated	guilty	happy
helpless	hopeful	hostile	humiliated	hurt	hysterical	innocent
interested	jealous	lonely	loved	lovestruck	mischievous	miserable
negative	optimistic	pained	paranoid	peaceful	proud	puzzled
regretful	relieved	sad	satisfied	shocked	shy	sorry
stubborn	sure	surprised	suspicious	thoughtful	undecided	withdrawn

Publisher: Wood 'N Barnes Publishing 800/678-0621

SECTION

Teaching Tales

THREE

THOUGHTS · NOTES · REVELATIONS

I have found the use of stories quite valuable in my work. Without fail, there is always a demand for more. In this section of **Teaching Tales** I have included some of my favorite stories. These stories can be used as metaphors to open the doors to discussion about different topics.

Recently, I discovered that "Bibliotherapy" is the term for the process of using stories with therapeutic intent. Through this technique, counselors can promote communication related to story topics and issues. For me, this establishes storytelling as a viable teaching tool (even though it has been for so long).

In the book "Biblio/Poetry Therapy" by Hynes & Hynes-Berry (1986), the authors state several important objectives related to choosing stories to read to clients.

- Stories should improve the capacity to respond by stimulating and enriching images and feelings.
- Stories should enhance value and personhood.
- Stories should enlighten interpersonal relationships.
- Stories should enlarge reality-orientation to the world we live in.

With these and your own program objectives in mind, choose stories that share a message and are interesting to listen to. You will want to keep in mind the mental age and maturity level of your group as well as their interests and experience.

The goal of the storyteller is to create emotion by bringing the story to life. "Tell" the story - try not to just read it. This may take a few practice runs in front of a mirror, but if you want to be good, practice.

When reading in front of others, use eye contact. This will give the audience the feeling that they are included in the story. Speak clearly and make sure that everyone can hear you. Also, use different voice tones and speeds to keep your listeners interested. Lastly, enjoy the story you are presenting. If it is not interesting to you, it will not be interesting to your audience.

I do hope you and yours enjoy the stories!

Author Unknown

How they frighten me.
Beginnings live at the bottom
and everything looks too big from the bottom.
Beginnings are clumpy and bumpy,
awkward and halting
too loud and boisterous, or too quiet and shy.

Beginnings are adolescents.
Big hands and feet that stride ahead,
and hearts that skitter and dart in fear and panic,
desperately looking for a fairy godmother,
who will turn them into
comfortable smooth middles or well-remembered ends.

Beginnings, I wish I could avoid you,
ignore you, pretend I don't need you.
I feel insecure, unsure of myself around you.
And yet, when I have rushed on past you,
I often look back and see how important, how exciting,
how dear you are to me.
For I need you, my beginnings,
to keep me growing - you are a part of me,
and if you all should leave me one day,
then my life would have less meaning.
Beginnings, you are so full of life.

DISCUSSION QUESTIONS:

- What has been a frightening beginning for you in the past? How did it turn out?
- Who remembers some of the feeling words in the passage? Discuss some of them. Did you relate to any of these feeling words? Explain.
- What is it like for you to start something new?
- What are your biggest fears when you start something new?
- What are you looking forward to in this program?
- What would your life be like without new beginnings? Would you give them up if you could?

(others)
-
-

THE UGLY BUG

Brian Brolin

While sitting beneath a tree
contemplating the many problems
that were grounding my spirit,
a bug flew by.

The bug was ugly and awkward,
frantically flapping its weird wings,
hardly keeping its scrawny body airborne.

I was snickering at the absurd insect
and its barely successful flight
when it changed course
and flapped nearer to me.

It hovered momentarily
and seemed to snicker at me
sitting there all ugly and absurd
and without wings.

DISCUSSION QUESTIONS:
- What do you think the lesson of the story is?
- What sort of things "ground your spirit"?
- Why did the man laugh at the bug?
- Why did the bug laugh at the man?
- Do you ever judge anyone before really getting to know them?
- What are some negative aspects of judging someone?
- Can you think of any positive aspects of judging someone?
- When you have troubles, do you ever make fun of others to forget about your trouble? Why do you think that is?
-
-

(others)

BIG JIM
Author Unknown

Smoke hung in the air like the steam from a locomotive. The bar was packed with travelers from far and wide, tossing back cold drinks on a hot summer day. From out of nowhere, a man came crashing through the door as if running for his life. "Big Jim is comin'," he screamed.

The momentary silence ended with a massive dash for every exit in the place. Not a chair left standing, every table overturned.

A few moments later, the sound of a mighty wind filled the air. The ground rumbled and the dust rose from its earthy bed. One side of the bar crashed in, exposing the misty sunlight.

A gigantic, red-bearded man riding a twelve-foot tall grizzly bear, using a chain for reins, and a live rattlesnake for a whip rode in and dismounted. "Give me a drink," the man roared. The remaining walls of the building shook like paper in the wind. Without a word, the bartender slowly placed a bottle of whiskey on the counter, slid it to the stranger, and returned to his shaded spot of protection behind the bar.

The tall man grabbed the bottle, drank the contents in one tremendous gulp, then chewed the bottle up and swallowed all the pieces. "Would...would you care for another?" stammered the shaded bartender. The large man shook his head, "Not for me," and remounted the grizzly. He took up the rattlesnake in one hand and ran the chains through the fingers of the other. "Don't have time for another drink. Ain't you heard? Big Jim's comin'."

DISCUSSION QUESTIONS:
- What did you think about the story?
- Did you think the red-bearded man was Big Jim? Why?
- Do you know what an assumption is? Do you think they're good or bad?
- Do you ever assume things about people?
- How can assumptions be harmful? Helpful?
- What kind of reputation do you think Big Jim has?
- What kind of reputation do you have ?
- Instead of assuming something about someone, what can you do?
- (others)
-

ACTIVITY: Cut 10-12 large pictures of people out of a magazine. Try to find a variety of expressions and scenes.

PROCEDURE: Before the story, show the group each picture. Have them describe to you what they think about the people in the picture based on the information they can see. Process with questions after the story.

PHILBERT

Chris Cavert

Did you know that all lizards are not lizards at all? It's true. Some lizards, we think are lizards, are actually shelless turtles. You didn't know turtles could leave their shells? Well they can. Here is a story of just such a turtle who did just that.

Philbert Bartholomew was the spunky new son of Delbert and Winney Bartholomew, often called Dell and Win. Philbert, who everyone called Phil, arrived in this world with more energy than anyone could believe a turtle could have - and a dash more.

One day while Phil and his father were out searching for breakfast, Phil asked, "What is this shell business all about? It always takes so long to get everywhere. I could do so much more if I didn't have one."

"It is in our nature to carry a shell," replied Philbert's father. "It protects us from being hurt, and it shelters us from the weather. Without our shells we would be vulnerable to the 'ways of the world.'"

Phil asked, "What are the 'ways of the world?'"

"Something you want to avoid at all cost," said his father and left it at that.

Since Phil didn't know the "ways of the world," he was not afraid but curious about them. However, he had this shell to contend with, and he wasn't going to find out the "ways of the world" with it slowing him down.

That night he wished upon the first star he saw, as many young turtles do. Phil wished to be free of his shell so he could find out for himself about the "ways of the world." Closing his eyes, Philbert Bartholomew fell asleep.

Sunshine broke over the horizon the next morning as it always did in Phil's neighborhood. Phil wiped the sleep from his eyes and noticed it was a bit chilly this particular morning. "A little early for fall," he thought and jumped to his feet to start a new day. Something was different. Phil couldn't quite figure it out yet, but something didn't seem right.

As Phil headed out for his morning meal, he noticed he was moving much faster than usual. His arms and legs felt much less constrained. He stopped in his tracks! "This can't be," said Philbert. He ducked his head inside his shell as he often did to shade the sun from his eyes, but there was no shade, THERE WAS NO SHELL! His wish had come true.

He dashed down the trail to the river. A trip that usually took all morning now took an instant. Phil was so excited. He turned around and headed back home as fast as he could.

Well, it was no surprise to find that everyone was surprised. Philbert was so excited to be without a shell. (He did find out, however, that his shell was still under the tree where he had slept the night before. This gave him a warm feeling inside, but he wasn't quite sure why.)

"I just came to say good-bye," Phil said. "I'm off to see the 'ways of the world.'" Even though all the other turtles encouraged Philbert to get back in his shell and stay away from the world, he turned his nose down the trail anyway and started out - much faster than any normal turtle would.

Philbert was off to see the "ways of the world." What do you think he saw? (I open up a discussion with the group at this point. I ask them to tell me what Philbert might see out there in the world. Group members often share personal experiences through Philbert's travels. This provides a good opportunity for discussion.)

Time and again Philbert would come back to visit his family and crawl, ever so gently, back into the protection of his shell - turtles need that sometimes you know. So if you ever see an empty turtle shell just lying around, please, don't pick it up. Some turtle, that we might think is a lizard, may need to get out of the rain someday.

DISCUSSION QUESTIONS:
- Have you ever felt like you were trapped inside of a shell - or held back by something? What did you do about it?
- Do you have a shell, of sorts, to protect you from the "ways of the world?" How do you act when you're in your shell?
- How do you know when you have to go into your shell? Do you tell anyone?
- Do you have a special place you consider your shell? Where is this place?
- Is there anyone or anything that makes you feel safe from the "ways of the world?" Could you share who or what that is?
- Have you ever wished for something? What was it? Have you gotten your wish yet? What would it take to have your wish come true?

(others)
-
-

(Keep a few notes from story discussions to share during future readings.)

73

SILVER BEAR'S DREAM

M. Marvin Lotz & Douglas Monahan.

Sleep had come to Silver Bear with great difficulty. For hours he had lain awake staring at the flickering shadows cast upon the walls of the tepee by the glowing embers of the slowly dying fire in the middle of the tepee floor. His mind was crammed with the memory of events that had occurred during the day. He had lost his temper and had said a great many things for which he was sorry; not just to one but to several of his best friends. His pride had kept him from apologizing, and yet he knew that he had been wrong. He wished with all his energy that the ugly words he had uttered might somehow be erased.

Finally he fell asleep. With the darkness that enveloped him came a dream. A dream in which a shadowy figure came to his tepee and spoke softly to him saying, "Silver Bear, we are preparing a message on our magic birchbark. We want you to read it carefully."

From out of nowhere the strange visitor produced a birchbark scroll and handed it to Silver Bear, as he continued, "All that you have said today, with never a word left out, has been written here. It will prove strange reading to you, no doubt. Before this night is over and this dream has come to an end, you will be forced to read the whole record through, for so the Great Spirit has commanded."

Silver Bear found a strange power forcing him to read the birchbark scroll. They were all there, the ugly words, all the foolish things he had said. He tried to force the sleep from himself and so avoid the accusing document, but he was held fast in its grip. There was no escape.

Hours passed, and as he scanned the final sheet of this strange scroll, Silver Bear was exhausted with the ordeal. He had no sooner read the last word than his strange visitor reappeared and spoke to him. "This has been a dream, Silver Bear, which we hope you will long remember. Its lesson is an important one; we hope you have clearly understood its meaning. If doubt lies in your mind, go to your father, Chief Flying Hawk, and he will help you understand."

With this message, the figure disappeared. Suddenly Silver Bear was awake. It was morning. His dream was over, but its impression remained strong in his mind. It was time to mend what had been broken.

DISCUSSION QUESTIONS:
- What do you think is the lesson to be learned from Silver Bear's strange dream.
- Have you said anything today that would have been better left unsaid?

•How does it make you feel when someone says unkind things to you?

•Do you think apologies make up for things that have been said?

•Have you ever been sorry for the things you have said? What did you do about it?

(others)

•

•

TWO BUCKETS

M. Marvin Lotz & Douglas Monahan.

Back in the days of the Old West, if you wanted to homestead your own land, you had to dig a well for your water supply. WELL, there was this particular well. It was deep, and its water was clear and cool. People came from miles around just to use this well. It had two buckets. When one bucket was lowered into the well, the other one would rise up from the depths. Always, one bucket came up while the other went down.

Now these buckets were not like most buckets, because they were heard to speak to each other on occasion. "I'm weary of this life," said one of the water containers one day. "No matter how many times I come up full, I always go down empty. I wish I had some other life."

The other bucket paused for a moment and replied, "I'm very happy, but then I look at my job differently from you. You say, no matter how many times you come up full you always go down empty, and you are discouraged. I say, no matter how many times I go down empty I always come up full of cool, refreshing water that many people need, and my job is an important and happy one. You see," said the bucket, "it all depends on how you look at it."

DISCUSSION QUESTIONS:
- What were some of the thoughts that ran through your mind as you listened to the story?
- What do you think it would have been like to live in the Old West?..and dig your own well (remember, no power tools)?
- Do you know anyone who resembles the weary bucket?
- Do you know anyone who resembles the happy bucket?
- What kind of bucket would you be?
- What lesson can be learned from this legend?
-
-

(others)

NOBODY KNOWS

Thanks to Brian Brolin.

Once upon a time in a faraway land, there was an old man. He lived in a small log cabin hidden deep in a dark forest. Nobody knew just where the cabin was, which was just the way the old man wanted it. Many others tried fruitlessly to find the place, but the old man told Nobody.

The old man had a special secret; he had a rainbow collection that was very dear to him, and he shared it with Nobody. It was a magnificent, magic collection of the most beautiful, real rainbows anyone could ever see. He had a whole bunch of little tiny ones - the kind you see on a sunny day when you throw water in the air. He had some tall, skinny ones that he found after light showers on Spring afternoons. And he had a huge, wide one that rose straight up from the ground like a pillar and disappeared into the clouds.

Nobody knew the value of the old man's rainbows and the great influence it could have on the rest of the world.

Nobody loved the old man, and the old man loved Nobody, so when it came time for the old man to die, he passed his rainbow collection on to Nobody. Nobody shared the magic and wonder of the rainbows with all the hopeless people. Nobody taught others the value and art of collecting rainbows.

Is this a happy story or a sad story? Nobody knows.

DISCUSSION QUESTIONS:
   •What do you think, is the story happy or sad? Why?
   •What or Who does the old man symbolize?
   •What do you think the rainbows symbolize? If you were the old man, what would your "rainbows" be?
   •What is the moral of the story? Does the moral change with how you read the story?
   •
   •

(others)

ACTIVITY: Brian suggests rereading the story, putting your name in place of "Nobody." He also has the group pass the story around the circle, each one reading aloud until they have inserted their name for the word "Nobody" once; then passing to the next person. Brian has observed powerful changes in groups as members read and realized their responsibility to carry on something positive.

To remember our experience, I provide crayons for drawing and coloring rainbows. Colors of a rainbow? Any color you want, but if you really need to know - ROY G. BIV: Red, Orange, Yellow, Green, Blue, Indigo, Violet.

LADYBUG & FROG

Thanks to Susana G. Acosta.

"Let's be friends," said the Ladybug one day.

"I can't," said the Frog, "I'll have to eat you for dinner."

"Why?" said the Ladybug who very seldom took "No" for an answer.

"Because," said the Frog, "that is what frogs do!"

"And what is that?" she said.

"EAT LADYBUGS!" shouted the Frog.

"Oh," said the Ladybug, giving some thought to his words. "Still," she said, "have you ever had a Ladybug friend? For sure you've had friends before, but have you ever had a Ladybug friend?"

"No," said the Frog, surprised at her question and her persistence. "Why would I want a Ladybug as a friend?"

"Well, Frog," said the Ladybug, "I could fly across the pond and bring you news from the other side. I could fan you with my wings when it gets hot. I could also scratch your back when you have an itch or tickle you when you are sad."

"Hmmm," croaked the Frog in contemplation. "And what would I have to do in return?" he asked. (He was a very practical frog and wanted to know what he was getting into.)

"Well," said the Ladybug. "You could sing to me as the sun goes down. You could tell me what it feels like to be under water. You could open and close your eyes very fast - I like to see you do that because I really like your eyes. But most of all, you could be my friend. We could be the first Frog and Ladybug friends in the entire valley."

Frog thought this to be an interesting proposal. He was kind of bored with the whole pond scenario anyhow and with some of the other frogs in general. So, even though it was not his idea initially, he was an adventurous frog and was willing to give it a try. "Okay," he said, "it's a deal. I promise not to eat you Miss Ladybug, and I'll try to be your friend. When do we start?"

Ladybug was so happy that she started fluttering about and slowly landed on Frog's head where she rested and softly whispered, "How about now my friend?"

"Well, okay then," said the Frog who started to sing his best evening song with a newfound joy in his heart.

As the sun went down, it seemed to Ladybug and Frog like they had been friends forever. "What a lovely voice you have Frog." she said softly. And with a little flutter of her wings, Ladybug quietly fell asleep feeling safe with her newfound friend. Safer than she had ever felt before.

DISCUSSION QUESTIONS:

- Who do you consider to be one of your friends? Why do you consider them your friend?
- What risk is there in having friends? What risk did Ladybug take? What risk did Frog take?
- What traits do you look for in a friend? What traits do you have as a friend?
- Have you ever tried making friends with someone that was new to your school/neighborhood/group? Was it easy or hard?
- Do you see yourself being more like the Ladybug or the Frog in the story?

(others)
-
-

The Giving Tree, Shel Silverstein.

The Missing Piece, Shel Silverstein.

The Fall of Freddie the Leaf, Leo Buscaglia.

Green Eggs and Ham, Dr. Seuss.

Oh the Places You Will Go, Dr. Seuss.

The Children's Book of Virtues, William J. Bennett. (A collection of short stories.)

Chicken Soup for the Kid's Soul, Jack Canfield, Mark Victor Hansen, Patty Hansen, & Irene Dunlap. (A collection of short stories.)

Chicken Soup for the Teenage Soul I & II, Jack Canfield, Mark Victor Hansen, Kimberly Kirberger. (A collection of short stories.)

SOME OF **M**Y **F**AVORITE "**L**ONGER" **S**HORT **S**TORIES:

Jonathan Livingston Seagull, Richard Bach.

Hope for the Flowers, Trina Paulus.

A Village Called Harmony, James Kavanaugh.

The Knight in Rusty Armor, Robert Fisher.

THOUGHTS · NOTES · REVELATIONS

SECTION FOUR

Minute Mysteries

THOUGHTS · NOTES · REVELATIONS

MINUTE MYSTERIES INTRODUCTION

Minute Mysteries can be tools for developing lateral and creative thinking during down times or transition periods to get the brain started. They provide a chance for groups to work cooperatively on a common problem and can promote feelings of group and individual success. Besides, they're great fun!

I have used Minute Mysteries successfully with groups 10 years of age and above. However, some Mysteries could be presented to younger groups. You won't know until you try.

The first time you present Minute Mysteries to a group, you will want to set some ground rules. You might start with something like this:

> "I would like to present you with a Minute Mystery. It will be your task to solve this mystery by asking me questions that I can answer with a 'yes' or 'no.' The only other answer I may use is, 'it doesn't matter.' I am willing to repeat the mystery if it will help you to hear it over."

Before you state the Mystery, ask the individuals who have heard the mystery before not to give away the answer if they know what it is. I often check their answer and, if they have it, I let them help me with the "yes" or "no" answers. A good esteem builder.

This is also a great teaching tool for promoting creative questioning. Try to encourage fact-finding questions as opposed to just asking "Is it a car?" Use a little body-language on the close questions to show the group you really want them to get it (sometimes I have been known to give a hint-but not always). There will also be times when you may want to stop and review what is already out on the table, since questions will start being repeated. (What could be said about listening?)

As with any activity, you don't want to "play it into the ground," so to speak. Present a Mystery, work on it for a while, then move onto something else if the group is unable to solve the problem right away. Assure them that you will continue to work on the problem later. Avoid relinquishing the answer. This can support giving up too soon. These Mysteries are great tools for working on persistence, patience and frustration levels (I could tell you stories).

There is grand processing potential with Minute Mysteries. Talking about the types of questions that are being asked, exploring feelings, and understanding what it takes to be successful are just a few concepts.

Check in with the participants who don't ask questions. Find out where they are. Can the group tell you how this type of questioning and thought processing could help them? There may also be the surprise issues that allow for great teach-able moments. (Don't we just love those?)

NOTE: Some of these Minute Mysteries involve death. Please be sensitive to the issues and maturity of your group when using such mysteries.

DOCTOR'S DILEMMA

From "Stories With Holes" by Irvington Publishers, Inc. (1981).

MYSTERY: A Doctor was driving his son to school one day when their car was rammed by a truck. The Doctor was found unconscious, and the son was seriously injured in the accident. They were both rushed to the hospital and the son was prepared for surgery. However, when they wheeled him into the room, the surgeon announced, "I can't operate! This is my son!" How is this so?

ANSWER: The surgeon was the boy's mother.

QUESTIONS:
- Why do we tend to assume doctors are men?
- What is an assumption? Are they good or bad?
- What gender do we usually see as doctors? What might be a reason for this? Is this good or bad?
- What is your feeling about women doctors? Should women be doctors? What would be a good reason to have a woman doctor?
- Why would the mother not want to operate on her son?
- Have you ever been in an accident?
- Do you know anyone that has been in a serious accident?
- Have you ever had an operation?
- What do you think about doctors? Do you trust them?
- Have you ever been in a hospital? How do you feel about hospitals?

(others)
-
-

MYSTERY: Two colleagues went out hunting. One was the father of the other one's son. How is this possible?

ANSWER: The two hunters are husband and wife.

QUESTIONS:
- What do we assume they are hunting for? Are there different types of hunting? Can you name some?
- What do you think about hunting? Have you ever been hunting?
- Why do we tend to think only men hunt? What do you think about women hunting?
- Can you think of any time in history or any group of people where women did the hunting (prehistoric times, some Amazon tribes)?
- What is a colleague? Do you have a colleague?
- Why do we assume colleagues are men?
- Can colleagues be married to each other? What would be some positives and negatives about this situation?
- How would you feel about being married to a colleague if she/he made more money than you did?

(others)
-
-

—A WALK IN THE RAIN—

MYSTERY: A woman left the building and started out on her short walk home. Suddenly, it began to rain. Even though she was totally unprepared for rainy weather, not a hair on her head got wet. Why not?

ANSWER: The woman was bald. (The building is a hospital. She is receiving chemo therapy treatment for cancer.)

QUESTIONS:
- What do you think about baldness? How would you feel being bald?
- What do you think about bald men?
- Have you ever seen a bald women? What was your first impression?
- What does having hair mean to you?
- Have you ever been around anyone that has lost their hair due to illness? How did it make you feel? Were you embarrassed to be around them?
- If you lost your hair, would you wear a hat? A wig? If you wore a wig, what hair color would you choose?
- Have you ever been out in the rain without an umbrella?
- Is rain a positive or a negative for you?
- If you had to get from one point to another and you had to go through the rain, would you get rained on more if you walked the distance or ran it?

(others)
-
-

89

MYSTERY: A woman lived on the twentieth floor of an apartment building. Every time she left her building, the woman would ride the self-service elevator from her floor down to the lobby. However, every time she returned, she rode the same elevator to the fifteenth floor where she got off and walked the stairs to the twentieth floor - unless it was raining. Then she rode all the way to her floor. What is the story?

ANSWER: The woman was a dwarf. She could not reach the button for her floor unless she brought an umbrella when it rained.

QUESTIONS:
   •What do you think about when you see someone different than you?
   •Have you ever seen a dwarf?
   •What do you think it is like for them?
   •What would you do if your parents were dwarfs?
   •What would you do if others made fun of them?
   •How do you think dwarfs feel?
   •Do you think that our cities are prepared for people that are "different"?
   •What changes would you make to improve the situation?
   •Have you ever lived in an apartment building?
   •What would you do if you were stuck in an elevator?

(others) •
   •

THE MAN IN THE MASK

MYSTERY: A young woman was afraid to go home because of the man in the mask. What is the situation?

ANSWER: The man is a catcher on a baseball team. The woman is a base runner.

QUESTIONS:
- Did you know that women are playing on college baseball teams?
- Is this okay?
- Why do you think there have not been women on baseball teams before?
- What other sports do you know women participate in?
- Can a woman be as good an athlete as a man?
- Name a sport that would not be appropriate for a woman?
- Why do you think this?
- Do you think women and men should play on the same team?
- Do you think only women are afraid?
- What are you afraid of?

(others)
-
-

PIERCING DILEMMA

Tim Finkbeiner

MYSTERY: A mother takes her small child to have her ears pierced. The mother decides that she would also like to get her ears pierced. However, the attendant states he cannot pierce the mother's ears. Why?

ANSWER: The mother is only 17 (or younger). She needs her mother's permission to get her ears pierced because she's under 18.

QUESTIONS:
- What are the responsibilities of a parent?
- What kind of parent do you think you could be right now?
- What would your life be like if you had a child?
- Do you have pierced ears?
- When did you get your ears pierced?
- Did you have a choice in the matter?
- What do you think about body piercing?
- What do you think about someone with a pierced eyebrow, nose or navel?
- Would others take you seriously?
- Do you think you would be able to find a job easily?
- What would you think if your mom or dad came home with a pierced nose?
-
-

(others)

MYSTERY: A team of archaeological explorers found two people frozen in a large chunk of ice. When they melted the ice away, the explorers knew exactly who the people were. Who were the people and how did they know?

ANSWER: Adam and Eve. They didn't have belly buttons.

QUESTIONS:
- What religion do you practice?
- What is your understanding of religion?
- Do you believe in God?
- Do you think that Adam and Eve really existed?
- Do you think that God created Adam first?
- Are you happy being a girl or a boy?
- In our society, do you think it is harder being a man or a woman?
- Would you be frozen for a hundred years and then come back?
- What changes do you think you would find?
- Would man still be on Earth?

(others)
-
-

ALBATROSS SOUP

From "Stories With Holes" by Irvington Publishers, Inc. (1981).

MYSTERY: Horton walked into a restaurant and read the menu - albatross soup. "My favorite!" he cried and ordered a double portion. The waiter brought the soup, and when Horton tasted it he screamed and fainted. Why?

ANSWER: Horton had once been a sailor. His ship was wrecked on a small island. (The same one Alan, Brad, and Chris were on - a different time, however.) One by one the crew died, but the captain kept the survivors alive until help came by feeding the men what he called "albatross soup." Horton realized in the restaurant - through the greatly different taste of the real albatross soup - that he had once eaten human flesh.

QUESTIONS:
- What would you do in the same situation?
- What would be important to you in such a situation?
- Do you know what "cannibalism" means?
- Do you think there are people on Earth that still practice cannibalism?
- Would you be able to eat human flesh if your life depended on it?
- Do you think you would rather die?
- If you were lost or stranded in a city, what would you do?
- If you were lost in the mountains, what would you do?
- Would you eat a snake or a worm?
- What do you think of people that eat dog, cat or frogs?
- What makes it different than eating chicken or beef?

(others)
-
-

MYSTERY: A man and a woman are quietly reading together. The woman gets up and turns out the light. The man continues to read. How is this possible?

ANSWER: The man is blind and reading in Braille.

QUESTIONS:
- What would it be like to be blind?
- Do you know a blind person?
- What is their life like?
- Have you ever seen the dog of a blind person?
- Do you like dogs?
- Do you know what Braille is?
- Do you know who invented it?
- What other method would you use to read if you were blind?
- Do you think that you could ride a bike or rollerblade?
- Have you ever closed your eyes and tried to move around your room?

(others)
-
-

FIVE MEN

MYSTERY: Five men were proceeding together down a country path. It began to rain. Four men quickened their step and began to walk faster. The fifth man made no effort to move any faster. (However, he remained dry and the other four got wet.)* They all arrived at their destination together. How could this be so?

*Add this part to made it a bit easier.

ANSWER: The four men were carrying the fifth - deceased man - in a coffin.

QUESTIONS:
- What are your feelings about dying?
- Did you ever know someone who died? How did you feel?
- How do you feel about all the violence that goes on today?
- When you die, would you prefer to be cremated or buried?
- Have you heard about people being buried alive?
- What way of dying do you think would be best?
- Which would be the worst?
- Would you rather die young or old?
- What do you think about suicide?
- How do you feel about the violence in the world today?
-
-

(others)

"Five Men" used with permission of Sterling Publishing Co., Inc., 387 Park Ave. S., NY, NY 10016 from LATERAL THINKING PUZZLERS by Paul Slone, ©1991 by Paul Slone.

Note: For more of these types of conundrums, look for the games, MindTrap and MindTrap II at your local games store or write to:

Great American Puzzle Factory
16 South Main St.
Norwalk, CT 06854

Another great resource is the MindWare catalog. They have a plethora of "Lateral Thinking" books and games. My favorite is MindTrek. They also have the MindTraps. Call 1-800-999-0398 for a catalog.

SECTION FIVE

Are You More Like...?

THOUGHTS · NOTES · REVELATIONS

—ARE YOU MORE LIKE...? INTRODUCTION—

Are you more like typing or writing? Are you more like reading or listening? If you look at these choices under the surface, you might find yourself searching for the meaning of life (or not). Anyway, this collection of options, if you will, started as Either/Or choices. A facilitator could use these choices with a group to show commonalities between group members; a way to get people to know each other a little better. In addition, the choices made by the participants can be used by the facilitator to split the group and direct them to a new activity. When the facilitator stumbles onto a choice that splits the group into the desired numbers, then off they go to discover new worlds.

The collection of possible proverbial pairs that follows can be used in a number of ways. Most of my younger friends like to choose the word they "like" or "prefer" the most. My older friends and I like to look at what the words represent to us, thus projecting this representation upon ourselves (I'm in a very therapeutic mood today). The facilitator could also ask additional questions about a choice that the participants have made.

I guess what I'm trying to tell you here is, I can only offer suggestions and ideas from my experiences with groups. This activity, like most others in this book, requires but is not limited to your creativity. Take it in whatever direction it goes. Because the bottom line is, as always, to coin a phrase, to sit where the sun shines, or to buy a postcard on vacation - in other words, have fun with them. It's the only reason I do this stuff.

ARE YOU MORE LIKE...

games for group • book 1

1. daisies or roses?

2. chocolate or strawberries?

3. a screen or a wooden door?

4. a carpet or a wooden floor?

5. skis or a snowboard?

6. a chain lock or dead bolt?

7. a glider or a 747?

8. Aspen, Colorado or Orlando, Florida?

9. a hard cover or paperback book?

10. roller blades or roller skates?

11. skim milk or 2%?

12. East or West?

13. a chair or a couch?

14. peppermint or spearmint?

15. a bulb or tube lighting?

16. North or South?

17. parking near the door or far away?

18. a candle or a flashlight?

19. a lemon or a lime?

20. apples or oranges?

21. pants or shorts?

22. blonde or brunet hair?

23. a hot springs or a Jacuzzi®?

24. a bath or a shower?

25. a beanbag chair or a Lazyboy®?

26. leather or Lycra®?

27. a donkey or a horse?

28. cloth or paper napkins?

29. dishwasher or hand washer?

30. Dijon® or yellow mustard?

31. American or Swiss cheese?

32. cane sugar or Equal®?

33. a crumpler or a folder?

34. a clothesline or a dryer?

ARE YOU MORE LIKE...

35. baked or french-fried potatoes?

36. bacon or sausage?

37. a backpack or a briefcase?

38. jeans or khakis?

39. baked or fried?

40. cherry or apple pie?

41. left or right?

42. down or up?

43. lobster or shrimp?

44. hard boiled or scrambled eggs?

45. sunny side up or sunny side over eggs?

46. caffeinated or decaffeinated?

47. A's or B's?

48. a cap or a hat?

49. blocks or legos?

50. concrete or wood?

51. glass or plastic?

52. a bunk bed or a twin bed?

53. a bus or a plane?

54. less or more?

55. a clock or a wristwatch?

56. a nose ring or a toe ring?

57. a bow tie or a neck tie?

58. a bracelet or a necklace?

59. a campfire or a fireplace?

60. a stander or a sitter?

61. solids or stripes?

62. the desert or the jungle?

63. sandals or shoes?

64. fleece or leather?

65. ruled or unruled paper?

66. baby blue or Navy blue?

67. a sailor or a soldier?

ARE YOU MORE LIKE...

68. a tropical island or a glacier?

69. the shade or the sun?

70. cursive or printing?

71. heads or tails?

72. a bikini or a one piece?

73. a speedo or trunks?

74. an organ or a piano?

75. a fiddle or a violin?

76. the drums or a tambourine?

77. bells or whistles?

78. a clap or a snap?

79. clockwise or counterclockwise?

80. a roller coaster or a merry-go-round?

81. digital or analog?

82. buttered or plain popcorn?

83. potato chips or pretzels?

84. cookies or rice cakes?

85. a run or a walk?

86. soda or water?

87. lip gloss or lip stick?

88. blue or green?

89. buttons or snaps?

90. Velcro® or zippers?

91. the sneak preview or the video?

92. gel or mousse?

93. panic or relaxed?

94. gel or paste?

95. cologne or perfume?

96. the back or the front?

97. the bottom or the top?

98. ground beef or a T bone?

99. diamonds or pearls?

100. a mobile phone or public phone?

ARE YOU MORE LIKE...

101. a weekday or a weekend?

102. Chick- Fill-A® or McDonalds®?

103. an elevator or an escalator?

104. long hair or short hair?

105. an essay or a poem?

106. fact or fiction?

107. Goofy® or Scoobydoo®?

108. Bullwinkle® or Rocky®? (the Moose or the Squirrel)

109. Barney Rubble® or Fred Flintstone®?

110. Air mail or E mail?

111. the Flintstones® or the Jetsons®?

112. Spiderman® or Superman®?

113. Bugs Bunny® or Daffy Duck®?

114. the Wiley Coyote® or the Roadrunner®?

115. Batman® or Robin®?

116. Cat Woman® or Wonder Woman®?

117. Oakleys® or Ray Bands®?

118. a plain cone or waffle cone?

119. bar soap or liquid soap?

120. liquid or powdered detergent?

121. peanut or plain?

122. contacts or glasses?

123. rain or shine?

124. a cat or a dog?

125. an oak or a willow tree?

126. salted or unsalted?

127. a broom or a vacuum?

128. the escalator or the stairs?

129. a bun or a loaf?

130. a chocolate or oatmeal cookie?

131. cheerios or corn flakes?

132. snow skiing or water skiing?

133. a passenger or a pilot?

ARE YOU MORE LIKE...

134. an aisle or a window seat?

135. plaid or stripes?

136. cotton or silk?

137. boxers or briefs?

138. country or rock and roll?

139. the ocean or a river?

140. the moon or the sun?

141. the beach or the mountains?

142. a pen or a pencil?

143. black or white?

144. a green light or a red light?

145. diamonds or hearts?

146. a hiking trail or a sidewalk?

147. fish or steak?

148. a Harley Davidson® or a Ninja® motorcycle?

149. hot or mild sauce?

150. a Ferrari or a Cadillac?

151. a desk top or a lap top computer?

152. pierced earrings or clip-ons?

153. 7 Up® or Sprite®?

154. Coke® or Pepsi®?

155. a gas or a wood-burning fireplace?

156. a conventional oven or a microwave?

157. diet or regular?

158. Tupperware® or Ziplocks®?

159. paper or plastic?

160. coffee or tea?

161. pasta or rice?

162. cheese or pepperoni?

163. indoors or outdoors?

164. hamburgers or hotdogs?

165. catsup or mustard?

166. flats or high heels?

ARE YOU MORE LIKE...

167. the rose or the thorns?

168. a belt or suspenders?

169. a passer or a belcher?

170. an ant or a grasshopper?

171. a 3-ringed binder or a spiral notebook?

172. wheat or white bread?

173. a cow or a horse?

174. a chapter book or a picture book?

175. fingers or toes?

176. rain or sunshine?

177. the future or the past?

178. an acoustic or electric guitar?

179. a cassette tape or a CD?

180. pig out or work out?

181. ice cream or yogurt?

182. a rectangular table or a round table?

183. animals or plants?

184. a marker or a pen?

185. a big screen or a small screen?

186. pancakes or waffles?

187. combat boots or cowboy boots?

188. sack lunch or school lunch?

189. the moon or the sun?

190. the circus or the zoo?

191. an amusement park or a water park?

192. a dolphin or a shark?

193. a honey bee or killer bee?

194. dark chocolate or white chocolate?

195. candy or popcorn?

196. fishing or hunting?

197. a cave or a tree house?

198. a hard hat or a top hat?

199. the basement or an attic?

ARE YOU MORE LIKE...

200. jacks or marbles?

201. checkers or chess?

202. ankle socks or knee socks?

203. a button shirt or a T-shirt?

204. a paper cup or a plastic cup?

205. a paper bag or a plastic bag?

206. fruits or vegetables?

207. a chalkboard or a white board?

208. a student or a teacher?

209. a listener or a talker?

210. a foot or a meter?

211. highlight or underline?

212. a square or a circle?

213. an answer or a question?

214. land or sea?

215. cable or satellite?

216. a long or mini skirt?

217. a snake or a spider?

218. the mud or the sand?

219. oil or vinegar?

220. tan or white?

221. "A" or "Z"?

222. a dark cloud or a white cloud?

223. a snow angel or a snow man?

224. skis or a sleigh?

225. downhill or uphill?

226. a globe or a map?

227. letters or numbers?

228. shoes or socks?

229. married or single?

230. a duffel bag or a trunk?

231. an electric shaver or a razor?

232. Romeo and Juliet or Star Wars®?

ARE YOU MORE LIKE...

233. a magazine or a newspaper?

234. a park or a playground?

235. automatic or manual transmission?

236. 2 or 4 wheel drive?

237. a climber or digger?

238. a one-way street or a two-way street?

239. playhouse or a tree house?

240. Art or Mathematics?

241. a tame horse or a wild horse?

242. a birthday or Christmas?

243. a paint gun or a water gun?

244. a bagel or a donut?

245. the mountains or the ocean?

246. an apartment or a house?

247. curly or straight?

248. a country road or the highway?

249. a convertible or a minivan?

250. stop or yield?

251. hide or seek?

252. a floppy disk or a hard drive?

253. typing or handwriting?

254. listening or reading?

255. cake or pie?

256. round or square?

257. plastic or sterling silverware?

258. caller ID or an answering machine?

259. cash or charge?

260. a card or a note?

261. a canoe or a kayak?

262. a camper or a tent?

263. a checking or savings account?

264. check-in or carry-on?

265. a knight or a peasant?

ARE YOU MORE LIKE...

266. a jester or a king?

267. crayons or paint?

268. Dennys® or McDonalds®?

269. a documentary or a safari?

270. a fountain or a spring?

271. a mountain climber or a spelunker?

272. a carport or a garage?

273. a foot or a hand?

274. a double black diamond or a green run?

275. a getter or a giver?

276. loud or quiet?

277. rope or string?

278. balancing or juggling?

279. one way or round trip?

280. carry out or dine in?

281. delivery or pick up?

282. a cardboard box or a plastic container?

283. a mountain bike or a road bike?

284. motor cross or street racer?

285. ice skates or roller blades?

Add your own:

Add your own...Submit your ideas of more "Are you more like..." for a future publication to:
Mony Cunningham, Wood 'N' Barnes Publishing, 2717 NW 50th, OKC, OK 73112

ARE YOU MORE LIKE...

Add your own...Submit your ideas of more "Are you more like..." for a future publication to:
Mony Cunningham, Wood 'N' Barnes Publishing, 2717 NW 50th, OKC, OK 73112

ARE YOU MORE LIKE...

Add your own...Submit your ideas of more "Are you more like..." for a future publication to:
Mony Cunningham, Wood 'N' Barnes Publishing, 2717 NW 50th, OKC, OK 73112

REFERENCES

Brolin, B. 709 S. 9th, Atchison, KS 66002 (913) 367-5085

Cain, J. & Jolliff, B. (1998). *Teamwork & teamplay.* Dubuque, IA: Kendall/ Hunt. (800) 228-0810.

Hanes, A. M., & Hynes-Berry, M. (1986). *Biblio/Poetry therapy: The interactive process.* Westview Press.

Harris, F. (1990). *Great games to play with groups.* Parsippany, NJ: Fearon Teacher Aids.

Hazel, William M., Center For Active Education, P.O. Box 2055, Warminster, PA 18974-0006.

Irvington Publishers, Inc. (1981). *Stories with holes.* Hightstown, NJ: N.L. Associates.

Knapp, C. E. (1988). *Creating humane climates outdoors: A people skill primer.* Charleston, WV: Appalachia Educational Laboratory.

Lotz, M. M., & Monahan, D. (1950). *Twenty tepee tales.* Out of print. (No copyright holder found).

McDowell, B., 373 W. Nees #219, Fresno, CA 93711.

The me I see: Answering life's questions (Journal) by Wood & Barnes Publishing Staff. Oklahoma City, OK: Wood & Barnes Publishing. (800) 678-0621.

Rohnke, K. (1994). *The bottomless bag again.* Dubuque, IA: Kendall/ Hunt.

Schoel, J., Prouty, D., & Radcliffe, P. (1988). *Islands of healing: A guide to adventure based counseling.* Hamilton MA: Project Adventure.

Sikes, Sam. (1999). *Executive marbles: And other team building activities.* Tulsa, OK: Learning Unlimited Corp.

Nadler, R. S., & Luckner, J. L. (1992). *Processing the adventure experience.* Dubuque, IA: Kendall/Hunt.

Wall, J., DeLano, W., & Delano, C. (1991). *Ropes course procedure manual.* Pittsboro, NC: Outdoor Institute.

THOUGHTS · NOTES · REVELATIONS

APPENDIX

APPENDIX

EXPERIENTIAL/ADVENTURE-BASED TRAINING COMPANIES

The companies listed here can provide staff training in the experiential process. I have noted which companies can provide training at your site and which companies provide training in a workshop setting throughout the country.

Chris Cavert
can be contacted through Wood 'N' Barnes Publishing (800) 678-0621

Trainings provided on site for,
the E.A.G.E.R. Curriculum,
Games (& other stuff) for Group • Book 1,
Games (& other stuff) for Group • Book 2,
Games (& other stuff) for Teachers,
Affordable Portables,
50 Ways to Use Your Noodle: Games with Foam Noodle Toys,
Low Ropes Facilitation, and High Ropes Skills and Facilitation.

Leahy & Associates, Inc.
1052 Artemis Circle, Lafayette, CO 80026 (303) 673-9832

Adventure-Based Training, Challenge Course Building & Development,
Challenge Facilitator Training, Risk Management & Operations.

Jim Cain
468 Salmon Creek Road, Brockport, New York 14420 (716) 637-0328
teamplay@frontiernet.net

Challenge and Adventure Activities, Staff Development and Training, Design and Engineering Analysis of Challenge Course Equipment.

Sam Sikes
Learning Unlimited, 5155 East 51st, Suite 108, Tulsa, OK 74135
(888) 622-4203
www.learningunlimited.com

Program Development, Staff Training, Activity Specialist.

Project Adventure
P.O. Box 100, Hamilton, MA 01936 (508) 468-7981

Trainings provided in workshop format
throughout the country. Call for catalog and schedule.

Donaldson, F. O., (1993). *Playing by heart: the vision & practice of belonging.* Deerfield Beach, FL: Health Communications, Inc..

Gil, E. (1991). *The healing power of play.* New York: Guilford Press.

Lawson, C. S., (1996). *The power of play: New visions of creativity.* West Chester, PA: Chrysalis Books.

Moe, J., & Pohlman, D. (1989). *Kids' power: Healing games for children of alcoholics.* Deerfield, FL: Health Communications.

Moore, G. B. (1988). *Learning: Becoming whole through games.* Atlanta, GA: Tee Gee Publishing.

Schaefer, C. E., & Reid, S. E. (Eds.). (1986). *Game play: Therapeutic use of childhood games.* New York: John Wiley & Sons.

Webb, N.B. (1991). *Play therapy with children in crisis.* New York: Guilford Press.

Association

Association for Play Therapy
c/o California School of Professional Psychology
1350 M Street, Fresno, CA 93721

Additional Information

Center for Play Therapy
University of North Texas
P.O. Box 13857
Denton, TX 76203-3857
(817) 565-3857
Dr. Garry Landreth, Director

Graduate Courses and Summer Institute
Workshops in Play Therapy.

Gopher Sport
2929 West Park, Owatonna, MN 55060
(800) 533-0446

Sportime
(800)283-5700

Flaghouse
150 NO. Macquesten Pkwy., Mt. Vernon, N.Y. 10550
(914) 699-1900 · (800) 221-5185

U.S. Game
(800) 327-0484

Mark One
924 W. 17th St., Bloomington, IN 47404
(800) 869-9058

World Wide Games
P.O. Box 517, Colchester, CT 06415-0517
(800) 243-9232

Bavarian Gaming Society
P.O. Box 9746, Brea, CA 92622-9746
(800) 247-3341

Bits & Pieces
The Great International Puzzle Collection
1 Puzzle Place B8016, Stevens Point, Wisconsin 54481-7199
(800) JIGSAWS
(fun games too)

Games Magazine
P.O. Box 605, Mount Morris, IL 61054-7789
(six magazines per year)

Flying Apparatus Catalogue
(415) 424-0739
(products from Klutz Press)

Chiji Processing Cards. The Institute for Experiential Education, 115 Fifth Ave. South, Suite 430, LaCrosse WI 54601. (608) 784-0789. (These cards can help aid in processing activities and are a fun way to build creativity and group discussions. Send $15.95 plus $3 for shipping.)

Biffle, C. (1990). *The Castle of the Pearl.* New York: Harper & Row.

Bristol, Hollace L. *The "I really like it when you" cards.* Dubuque, IA: Kendall/ Hunt. (800) 228-0810. www.kendallhunt.com

Eckert, L. (1998). *"If anybody asks me...1001 focused questions for educators, counselors, and therapists"* Oklahoma City, OK: Wood & Barnes Publishing. (800) 678-0621.

Feelings Market Place Cards (youth and adult decks). Project Adventure, P.O. Box 100 Hamilton, MA (508) 468-7981.

Jackson, T. *More Activities That Teach.* Call Tom at (435) 586-7058

Jackson, T. (1993). *Activities That Teach.* Call Tom at (435) 586-7058

O'Conner, K. (1983). The color-your-life technique. In Schaefer, C., & O'Conner, K. (Eds.). *Handbook of play therapy.* New York: Wiley.

Stock, G. *The Kids Book of Questions.*

Stock, G. (1987). *The Book of Questions.* New York: Workman Publishing.

THOUGHTS · NOTES · REVELATIONS

THOUGHTS · NOTES · REVELATIONS

THOUGHTS · NOTES · REVELATIONS

THOUGHTS · NOTES · REVELATIONS

THOUGHTS · NOTES · REVELATIONS